# Spills and Ripples

**Authors**
Robert F. Benjamin
Jim Wilson
Dave Youngs

**Editor**
Betty Cordel

THE GLENN T. SEABORG CENTER
West Science
Northern Michigan University
Marquette, MI 49855
(906) 227-2002

**Illustrator**
Brenda Richmond

**Desktop Publisher**
Tracey Lieder

Activities Integrating
AIMS
Math, Science, & Technology

**Los Alamos**
NATIONAL LABORATORY

D1708016

This book contains materials developed by the AIMS Education Foundation. AIMS (Activities Integrating Mathematics and Science) began in 1981 with a grant from the National Science Foundation. The non-profit AIMS Education Foundation publishes hands-on instructional materials (books and the monthly magazine) that integrate curricular disciplines such as mathematics, science, language arts, and social studies. The Foundation sponsors a national program of professional development through which educators may gain both an understanding of the AIMS philosophy and expertise in teaching by integrated, hands-on methods.

ISBN 1-881431-83-5

Printed in the United States of America

I Hear and I Forget,

I See and
   I Understand,

I Do and I Remember.

—Chinese Proverb

iii

# Table of Contents

Preface ............................................................................................. viii
Los Alamos National Laboratory ........................................................ ix
An Overview of Spills and Ripples .................................................... x
Who Cares About Rayleigh-Taylor Instability? ................................... 1
Science Research as Toddler's Play ................................................... 3
Density .............................................................................................. 5
Pressure ............................................................................................ 6
Confusing Measurements and Units of Pressure ............................... 7
Surface Tension ................................................................................ 11
Two Oceans ...................................................................................... 13
Betwixt and Between ........................................................................ 14

## Rayleigh-Taylor Instability

Look Out Below! ............................................................................... 18
Sauces ............................................................................................... 24
Trickle Triathlon ............................................................................... 26
Flow Fingers ..................................................................................... 36
Fluid Instabilities and Complexity .................................................... 41
Liquid Rope ...................................................................................... 42
A Fluid-Dynamical Centerpiece ........................................................ 46
Soapy Spills ...................................................................................... 47
Brackish Water .................................................................................. 52
The Solar Pond .................................................................................. 57
Mixing ............................................................................................... 59
Oopsy Do .......................................................................................... 60
Wet Papers ........................................................................................ 64

## Basic Fluid Properties

Density Dealings ............................................................................... 65
Hippo Hydrometer ............................................................................ 70
Hydrometer Applications .................................................................. 78
A Density Puzzler .............................................................................. 79
Open-tube Manometer ...................................................................... 80
Water Pressure Applications ............................................................. 87
A Penny for Your Drops .................................................................... 88
Measuring Drops on a Penny ............................................................ 95
Pennies in a Cup ............................................................................. 102
More Pennies in a Cup ..................................................................... 105
Delicate Diver .................................................................................. 109
The Diver's Dilemma: Submarine or Sea Animal? ........................... 114
How do Sea Animals Dive to Depths of Several Hundred Meters? .... 117
The Science and Engineering of The Diver's Dilemma ..................... 119
The Reverse Diver ............................................................................ 120
Archimedes ..................................................................................... 124
Soda Can Dunk ............................................................................... 126
Geoffrey I. Taylor (1886-1977) ........................................................ 133
Lord Rayleigh (John William Strutt, 1842-1919) ............................. 134
Professor Sheila Widnall (1938-    ) ................................................. 135
Glossary .......................................................................................... 136

# ANNOTATED TABLE OF CONTENTS

WHO CARES ABOUT RAYLEIGH-TAYLOR INSTABILITY?...........................................1
celebrating the reasons why Rayleigh-Taylor Instability is terrific for science education

SCIENCE RESEARCH AS TODDLER'S PLAY .............................................3
examining strong similarities between behaviors of toddlers and scientists

BASICS OF FLUIDS
    DENSITY ...........................................................................5
    PRESSURE.........................................................................6
    SURFACE TENSION .........................................................11
explaining the fundamental properties of fluids

TWO OCEANS.........................................................................13
recognizing that we live at the bottom of the atmosphere and top of water oceans

BETWIXT AND BETWEEN.......................................................14
focusing on interfaces and boundaries as the sites where much science occurs

## RAYLEIGH-TAYLOR INSTABILITY SECTION

LOOK OUT BELOW!.................................................................18
controlling ripples to keep water in an upside-down jar

TRICKLE TRIATHLON.............................................................26
determining the limits of spill-control by surface tension and porous barriers

FLOW FINGERS.....................................................................36
admiring beautiful flow patterns of fluid instabilities

LIQUID ROPE.......................................................................42
observing the steady flow that is started by fluid instability

SOAPY SPILLS.....................................................................47
investigating the spilling of soapy water, where ripples form more easily than freshwater

BRACKISH WATER ...............................................................52
studying fluid instability at interfaces of freshwater and saltwater

THE SOLAR POND ...............................................................57
suppressing fluid instability to harness solar energy

MIXING ...............................................................................59
considering various ways to mix two fluids

OOPSY-DO .........................................................................60
applying Rayleigh-Taylor Instability to evaluate the strength of wet paper

# BASIC FLUID PROPERTIES SECTION

DENSITY DEALINGS ..................................................................................65
creating a column of variable-density liquid to estimate the density of solids

HIPPO HYDROMETER ..............................................................................70
constructing and calibrating a hydrometer to measure the relative densities of liquids

OPEN-TUBE MANOMETER .......................................................................80
building a manometer to measure how water pressure changes with water depth

WET PENNIES
   A PENNY FOR YOUR DROPS.................................................................88
   MEASURING DROPS ON A PENNY ....................................................95
   PENNIES IN A CUP ................................................................................102
   MORE PENNIES IN A CUP ....................................................................105
quantifying surface tension and collecting lots of data

DELICATE DIVER .....................................................................................109
discovering how small changes in pressure and density sink the diver

THE DIVER'S DILEMMA ..........................................................................114
probing the difference between buoyancy controls of fish and submarines

THE REVERSE DIVER ...............................................................................120
squeezing a bottle to decrease pressure produces startling results

SODA CAN DUNK ....................................................................................126
exploring floating, sinking, and Archimedes' principle

# BIOGRAPHIES

BIOGRAPHIES .....................................................................124,133-135
honoring some pioneer researchers in fluid instabilities

**Geoffrey I. Taylor**      **Lord Rayleigh**      **Professor Sheila Widnall**

Abbreviated descriptions of some Rayleigh-Taylor activities appeared in the cover article of "The Physics Teacher" magazine, September 1999, pages 332-336.

# APPLICATIONS AND PERSPECTIVES

WHO CARES ABOUT RAYLEIGH-TAYLOR INSTABILITY? ...................................... 1
considering the many reasons for studying fluid instability

SCIENCE RESEARCH AS TODDLER'S PLAY ................................................. 3
examining strong similarities between behaviors of toddlers and research scientists

TWO OCEANS ...................................................................................... 13
recognizing that we live at the bottom of the atmosphere and top of water oceans

SAUCES ............................................................................................... 24
observing that bottles are designed with fluid instability in mind

FLUID INSTABILITIES AND COMPLEXITY ................................................. 41
pondering the birth of a new branch of science

A FLUID-DYNAMICAL CENTERPIECE ...................................................... 46
creating an exquisite decoration using fluid instabilities

THE SOLAR POND ............................................................................... 57
harnessing solar energy by blocking Rayleigh-Taylor Instability

MIXING .............................................................................................. 59
recognizing three distinct methods of mixing liquids

WET PAPERS ...................................................................................... 64
engineering papers to perform certain tasks while soggy

HYDROMETER APPLICATIONS .............................................................. 78
applying a hydrometer to car batteries, maple syrup, and more

WATER PRESSURE APPLICATIONS ........................................................ 87
constructing a large dam

THE DIVER'S DILEMMA: SUBMARINE OR SEA ANIMAL? ........................ 114
puzzling about buoyancy control in technology and animals

HOW DO SEA ANIMALS DIVE TO DEPTHS OF SEVERAL HUNDRED METERS? .............. 117
diving with controlled density instead of active propulsion

THE SCIENCE AND ENGINEERING OF THE DIVER'S DILEMMA ....................................... 119
examining how science supports engineering and how they are different

# Preface

# The Origin of Spills and Ripples

As a diligent parent volunteering in my children's classrooms, I had been searching for science demonstrations about the properties of fluids. As a research scientist at the Los Alamos National Laboratory (LANL), I had been studying fluid instabilities, a subject unknown to precollege education. Encouraged by colleagues, including Prof. Jeff Jacobs and Dr. Dave Sharp, I began developing classroom activities about Rayleigh-Taylor Instability. I began finding examples of it everywhere, even though it's little known. In addition to presenting classroom demonstrations for students, I gave workshops to high school teachers at "Science Teacher's Day" during various meetings of the American Physical Society, and I received a grant from the LANL Education Program Office to pursue this initiative as part of my job.

My wife Susan, an AIMS trainer, suggested I discuss these activities with Dave Youngs and Jim Wilson at AIMS. I did so and they enthusiastically endorsed a collaboration leading to several articles in the AIMS magazine and culminating in this book.

The collaboration nurtured the original concept far beyond fluid instabilities. Jim not only edited the Rayleigh-Taylor activities, but also developed a passion for the Cartesian Diver, another effect that depends on the interplay of density and pressure. He may now have the most extensive collection of Cartesian Divers on the planet. Dave critiqued the Rayleigh-Taylor activities, revived some wonderful activities on density and surface tension, and guided the project to a broader mission. Eventually the Spills and Ripples project shifted from a book about instabilities to a book about fluids and science-process skills, using Rayleigh-Taylor Instability as an innovative gateway to provoke curiosity, interest, and fun. This book is about the joy of learning physics in the kitchen sink and about realizing how much our daily lives are affected by fluid instability. Enjoy!

Robert F. Benjamin

**Los Alamos**
NATIONAL LABORATORY

The development and writing of *Spills and Ripples* has been partially supported by the Los Alamos National Laboratory and the U. S. Department of Energy. These two entities sponsored the participation of Dr. Robert Benjamin to develop the Rayleigh-Taylor Instability activities and much of the explanatory information contained in the book. Dr. Benjamin collaborated with staff members of the AIMS (Activities that Integrate Mathematics and Science) Education Foundation to write and publish this book.

The Laboratory's Education Program Office acts as "a bridge to the future" by encouraging strategic partnerships that connect students and faculty to premier research and learning opportunities. These partnerships strengthen the science and technology mission of the Lab. One clear example of a successful partnership is this collaboration between AIMS and Dr. Benjamin to develop classroom lessons that make fluid instabilities understandable to students, teachers, parents, and the public. The Laboratory hopes that *Spills and Ripples* proves to be an important and useful contribution to the national portfolio of curriculum materials for science educators.

# An Overview of *Spills and Ripples*

## Rayleigh-Taylor Instability

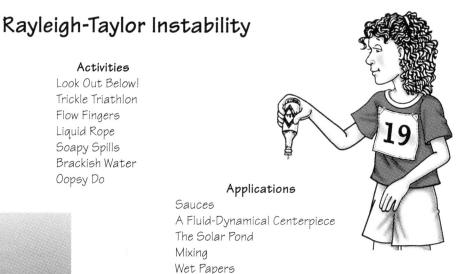

### Explanations
Science Research as Toddler's Play
Density
Pressure
Confusing Measurements and Units
    of Pressure
Surface Tension
Two Oceans
Betwixt and Between

### Activities
Look Out Below!
Trickle Triathlon
Flow Fingers
Liquid Rope
Soapy Spills
Brackish Water
Oopsy Do

### Applications
Sauces
A Fluid-Dynamical Centerpiece
The Solar Pond
Mixing
Wet Papers

## Basic Fluid Properties

### Activities
Density Dealings
A Penny for Your Drops
Measuring Drops on a Penny
Pennies in a Cup
More Pennies in a Cup

### Measurement Tools
Hippo Hydrometer
Open-tube Manometer

### Applications
Hydrometer Applications
Water Pressure Applications

## Cartesian Diver

### Activities
Delicate Diver
The Reverse Diver

### Applications
The Diver's Dilemma: Submarine
    or Sea Animal
How Do Sea Animals Dive to
    Depths of Several Hundred
    Meters?
The Science and Engineering of
    The Diver's Dilemma

# Who cares about Rayleigh-Taylor Instability?

A baby turns over a cup of milk and the milk spills all over the floor. River water flowing into an ocean mixes with the salty seawater. A couple at dinner shakes and then pours dressing on their delicious salads. A powerful underwater volcano spews hot liquids and gases upward through the ocean waters.

These seemingly unrelated events are all related to Rayleigh-Taylor Instability (RTI). We have all observed it unknowingly, yet few of us can identify it. It happens when a higher-density fluid finds itself above a lower-density fluid. When ripples form at the interface, they grow and grow. We usually observe spilling or mixing as a consequence. Rayleigh-Taylor Instability is the growth of ripples at an interface when a higher-density fluid is above a lower-density fluid. A useful example is an upside-down, uncovered jar of water, which has water (in the jar) above air (just under the jar). Students usually say that the water spills out because of gravity, and indeed gravity is part of the reason. But another effect, RTI, is also involved as we'll see in these activities.

*Spills and Ripples* is a collection of hands-on activities that encourages us to confront RTI. We not only learn to recognize it, but we also learn how to control it. Experiencing and controlling a fluid instability is an exciting challenge and a fun way to deepen our understanding of basic concepts in fluids, like pressure, density, and surface tension, which are major players in controlling RTI.

Rayleigh-Taylor Instability involves the delicate interplay of pressure, density, and surface tension at interfaces between fluids. It causes liquids and gases to mix in ways familiar to us. It is so common that we become startled when it does not occur, as we'll see in some *Spills and Ripples* activities.

Why should elementary and middle-school students study Rayleigh-Taylor Instability, an effect rarely mentioned in science texts? We offer seven reasons and you may know additional ones. First, it helps people to understand the everyday world. It affects weather patterns and ocean currents, as well as the spilling of water and the design of food bottles.

Second, many of the observations and data are visually striking. Rayleigh-Taylor Instability appeals to students with artistic inclinations who are less interested in numerical data. It draws these students to the study of fluids, and hopefully to science.

Third, it helps to clarify the concepts of density and pressure, which are elusive for many students, and are sometimes perceived as the same property. It demonstrates dramatically that the pressure of air around us is the same as the water pressure at the surface of water in a glass, even though the water is hundreds of times more dense than the air.

Fourth, it's enormous fun. Blocking Rayleigh-Taylor Instability provides the basis for amusing tricks. Students who become adept can show off to parents and friends. Students see a compelling relationship between understanding physics and influencing everyday phenomena.

Fifth, it demonstrates how an event can have predictable aspects and simultaneously unpredictable features. Thus it illustrates some fundamentals of the emerging science of "chaos," but without the math.

Sixth, it painlessly introduces the student to some essential notions in engineering. Students learn to observe and categorize different ways that a paper barrier can fail to confine water. These activities call attention to learning from events that don't yield the expected results. The lessons not only teach about fluids but also about properties of important materials, like water, air, and paper.

Seventh, Rayleigh-Taylor Instability demonstrates that physical properties of materials can have both static and dynamic effects. We usually associate density with buoyancy (whether an object floats or sinks) which is basically a static effect. Yet we learn from RTI that subtle density differences can have dramatic influences on the dynamics of flows and fluid mixing.

Anyone who cares about any of these benefits will enjoy learning about and controlling Rayleigh-Taylor Instability. This instability occurs at fluid interfaces, so we begin our investigation by developing a better awareness of interfaces all around us, particularly interfaces between fluids.

# Science Research as Toddlers' Play

Toddlers learn by answering their own unspoken questions. They observe an event that excites their curiosity and they devise experiments to explore and learn how it works. For example, the one-year-old that happens to knock a cup off a table will be impressed by the "Wham!" it makes upon impacting the floor. After the cup is returned to the table, the toddler will again knock it off, deliberately this time. Toddlers are usually willing to repeat this experiment far longer than a parent's patience to keep picking up the cup and replacing it on the table. The toddler has non-verbally asked a series of questions: Does the cup always hit the floor and make an exciting noise? Does the cup always fall down? The toddler conducts experiments to learn whether the answer is "yes" or "no" to each question.

Indeed, that is also the purpose of scientific experiments: to determine whether the answer to a question is yes or no. When an experiment yields the answer "maybe" or "sometimes," the result is less valuable than a simple yes or no. Learning to ask good questions and how to answer them takes practice. Scientists, like toddlers, need to develop two important skills: how to ask questions and how to answer questions. *Spills and Ripples* is intended to motivate the development of both of these skills. Because Rayleigh-Taylor Instability is usually unfamiliar to students (and teachers), they can improve their skill at asking yes-no questions about a new event, just as they did many years ago as toddlers.

Learning how to answer questions scientifically is the purpose of the scientific method. Before considering how to help students learn to answer questions, let's first consider how we teach students to ask questions. The non-verbal toddler is motivated to ask questions based on curiosity and wonder. The cup hit the floor and made a wonderful noise—will it happen again if I hit the cup again?

Older people ask questions for other reasons as well. Perplexing observations are good sources of questions. Watching a magic show prompts queries of "That's incredible! How could he possibly do that?" Becoming confused by apparently non-reproducible events, like weather, is another motivation. Mental models of how things work lead to questions, especially about events that are not consistent with the model. For example, people are accustomed to seeing water spill from a bottle when it is turned upside down. When an inverted, water-filled, sample-size bottle of mouthwash doesn't spill, the usual model of spilling seems inadequate. Consequently more questions come to mind: Is this the only bottle that holds in water when turned upside down? Does the bottle shape cause this to happen? Does the opening size matter? Will the water come out if the bottle is squeezed? These and other questions arise from an event that contradicts people's experience-based expectations.

*thunk!*

*Spills and Ripples* is about teaching students to ask questions about simple events involving water spills. The students are confronted with unusual events and offered a simple but unfamiliar idea that explains spilling. Students can then ask questions, which become experiments in *Spills and Ripples,* or they may ask questions that lead to other experiments. Teachers and students are encouraged to think carefully about their concepts of fluid pressure, density, surface tension, and interface, and then use these basic experiments as springboards to check out whether these concepts truly "hold water."

Back to the subject of answering scientific questions. The scientific method is simply a framework, a way, for doing this. It starts with a hypothesis, which is basically a question to be answered yes or no. As we know, much of the fun and excitement in science occurs in creating the hypothesis. Science doesn't begin with the hypothesis because we had to do a lot of thinking and observing in order *to* arrive at a hypothesis. The "hypothesis step" is somewhere in the middle—at the end of asking the question and the beginning of answering it. Modern science provides the discipline to move from framing the question to a decisive method for answering it.

The scientific method continues with the logical steps: design an experiment and gather needed materials; perform the experiment, preferably many times to learn about reproducibility and errors; make observations; then interpret the results; and draw conclusions. History tells us that this method of answering questions works effectively.

# Density

Density is a measure of the "compactness" of a material. It is the ratio of mass to volume for any material measured in grams per cubic centimeter (g/cm³) and tells how much matter is packed into a given space. Density is not a simple comparison of the "heaviness" or "lightness" of materials. It is instead, a comparison of the "heaviness" or "lightness" of the same amounts (mass per unit volume) of materials.

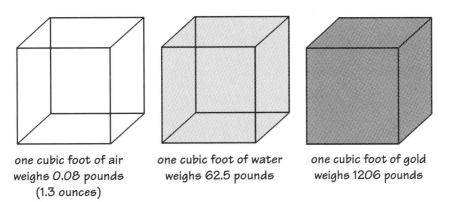

one cubic foot of air weighs 0.08 pounds (1.3 ounces)

one cubic foot of water weighs 62.5 pounds

one cubic foot of gold weighs 1206 pounds

A steel paper clip has the same density as a steel beam. The beam is thousands of times more massive than the paper clip, but it also takes up thousands of times more space, so the ratio of mass to volume (density) remains the same for both (about 7.8 g/cm³). The density of a small pebble is greater than the density of a huge redwood tree even though the tree is much larger. The density of a kilogram of feathers is much less than the density of a kilogram of gold even though they have the same mass. The mistake most people make in thinking about density is to consider only size or mass instead of both of them together. When dealing with density, mass and volume always go hand in hand.

The density of materials is determined by the masses of the atoms in the material and the amount of space between the atoms. Gases have a low density not only because the atoms making up the gases have a small mass, but also because there is a large amount of space between the atoms. The heavy metals like gold, lead, and uranium are very dense because the atoms they are composed of are massive and spaced closely together. The densest substance on Earth is osmium with a density of 22.6 g/cm³.

Water has a density of one gram per cubic centimeter at four degrees Celsius. It is the standard for comparing the density of materials. A block of any material with a density greater than one gram per cubic centimeter is denser than water and will sink. A block of any material with a density that is less will float. The force causing it to float is called buoyancy. (Buoyancy is discussed in the Cartesian Diver section of this book.) Lead has a density of 11.3 g/cm³ which tells us it is more than 11 times as dense as water. This means that a cup of lead would have more than 11 times the mass of a cup of water. It also means that 100 grams of lead would have more than 11 times less volume than 100 grams of water since the atoms in lead are much more closely packed together and take up less space.

# Pressure

The pressure concept is one you can literally get a feel for. A simple quantitative look at cube stacking is a way to develop the pressure concept.

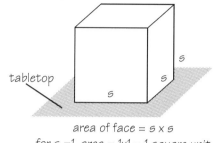

area of face = s x s
for s =1, area = 1x1 = 1 square unit

Consider a single cube sitting on the flat surface of a tabletop. The bottom face of the cube is the only part of the cube that is in contact with the table. The area of contact is simply the area of the bottom face of the cube. If s is the length of one side of the cube, then s x s is the area of the face in contact with the table.

For simplicity, let's consider a cube that has one unit of weight and one unit side length (the area of the face of the cube equals one square unit).

As the cube sits on the table (or the palm of your hand), it obviously *presses* on the table. The weight of the cube is evenly distributed over the area of contact between the bottom face of the cube and the table. The quantitative relationship between the weight of the cube and the area of contact is defined as *pressure* and can be expressed in equation form as

$$\text{pressure} = \frac{\text{weight}}{\text{area}}.$$

But weight is a *force* measure so the relationship may be more generally written as

$$\text{pressure} = \frac{\text{force}}{\text{area}}.$$

Therefore, the equation tells us that a cube with one unit of weight and a bottom face of one square unit of area will exert one unit of pressure on that one square unit of area.

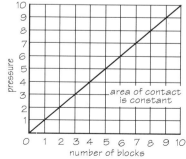

Now consider what happens if a second, identical cube is placed on top of the first cube. The area of contact between the cubes and the table hasn't changed, but the weight (force) has doubled. Therefore, the pressure at the bottom of the stack has doubled.

There's a direct relationship between the number of blocks in the stack and the pressure at the area of contact between the stack and tabletop. The following table and graph describe this relationship.

| # of blocks | 0 | 1 | 2 | 3 | 4 |
|---|---|---|---|---|---|
| pressure | 0 | 1 | 2 | 3 | 4 |

area of contact is constant

(graph: pressure vs. number of blocks)

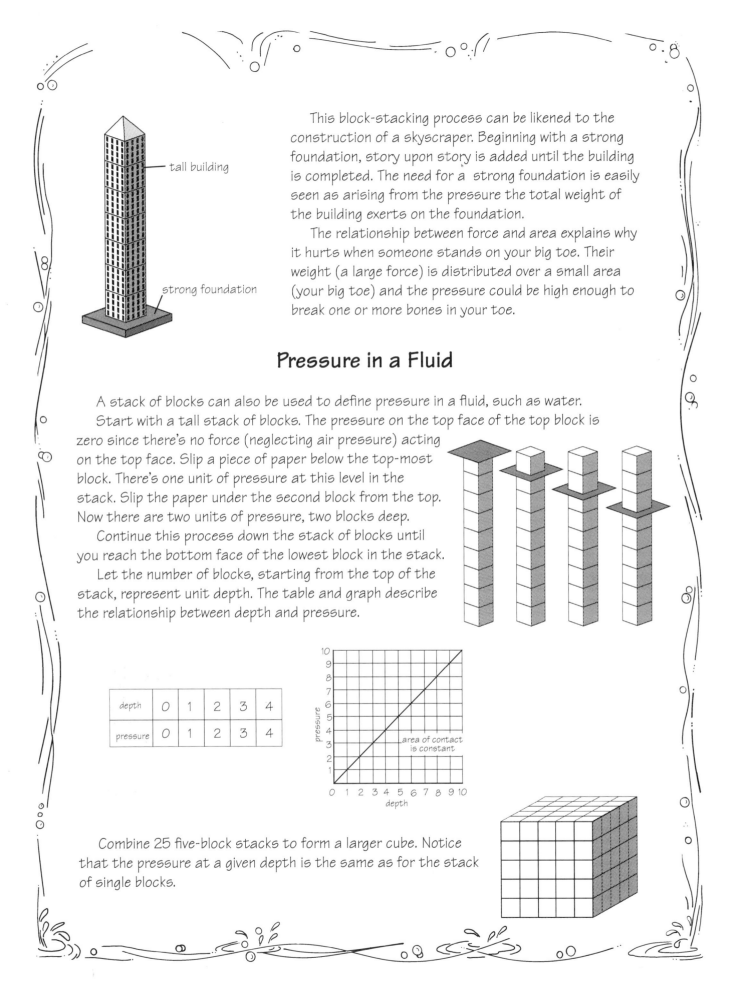

This block-stacking process can be likened to the construction of a skyscraper. Beginning with a strong foundation, story upon story is added until the building is completed. The need for a strong foundation is easily seen as arising from the pressure the total weight of the building exerts on the foundation.

The relationship between force and area explains why it hurts when someone stands on your big toe. Their weight (a large force) is distributed over a small area (your big toe) and the pressure could be high enough to break one or more bones in your toe.

tall building

strong foundation

## Pressure in a Fluid

A stack of blocks can also be used to define pressure in a fluid, such as water.

Start with a tall stack of blocks. The pressure on the top face of the top block is zero since there's no force (neglecting air pressure) acting on the top face. Slip a piece of paper below the top-most block. There's one unit of pressure at this level in the stack. Slip the paper under the second block from the top. Now there are two units of pressure, two blocks deep.

Continue this process down the stack of blocks until you reach the bottom face of the lowest block in the stack.

Let the number of blocks, starting from the top of the stack, represent unit depth. The table and graph describe the relationship between depth and pressure.

| depth | 0 | 1 | 2 | 3 | 4 |
|---|---|---|---|---|---|
| pressure | 0 | 1 | 2 | 3 | 4 |

area of contact is constant

Combine 25 five-block stacks to form a larger cube. Notice that the pressure at a given depth is the same as for the stack of single blocks.

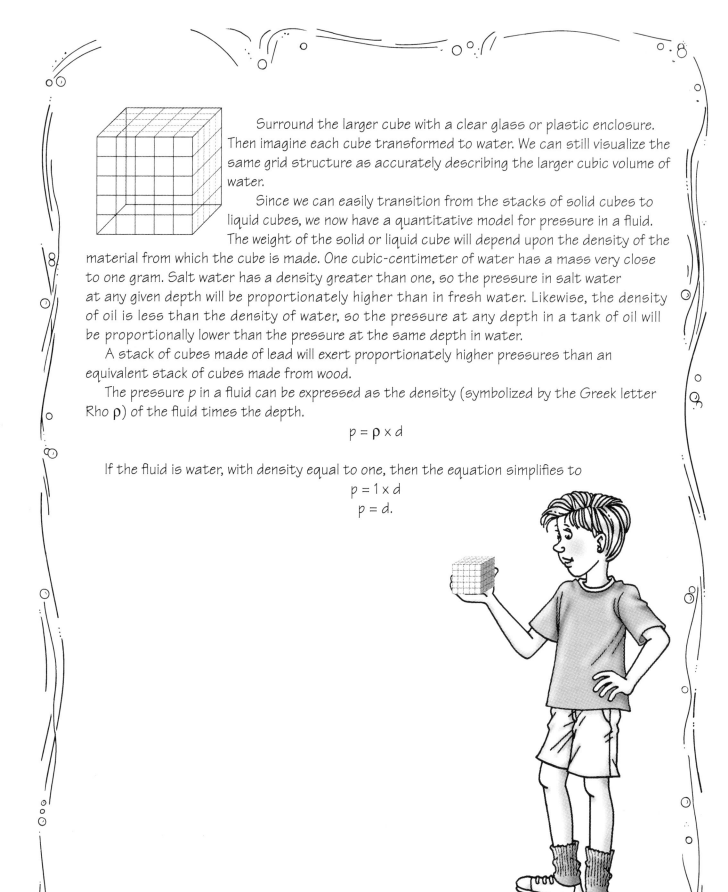

Surround the larger cube with a clear glass or plastic enclosure. Then imagine each cube transformed to water. We can still visualize the same grid structure as accurately describing the larger cubic volume of water.

Since we can easily transition from the stacks of solid cubes to liquid cubes, we now have a quantitative model for pressure in a fluid.

The weight of the solid or liquid cube will depend upon the density of the material from which the cube is made. One cubic-centimeter of water has a mass very close to one gram. Salt water has a density greater than one, so the pressure in salt water at any given depth will be proportionately higher than in fresh water. Likewise, the density of oil is less than the density of water, so the pressure at any depth in a tank of oil will be proportionally lower than the pressure at the same depth in water.

A stack of cubes made of lead will exert proportionately higher pressures than an equivalent stack of cubes made from wood.

The pressure $p$ in a fluid can be expressed as the density (symbolized by the Greek letter Rho $\rho$) of the fluid times the depth.

$$p = \rho \times d$$

If the fluid is water, with density equal to one, then the equation simplifies to

$$p = 1 \times d$$
$$p = d.$$

# Confusing Measurements and Units of Pressure

Among physical quantities that we encounter every day, like pressure, weight, and temperature, the measurements of pressure and the units for measuring pressure are probably the most confusing. We hear about pressure during weather reports, like "the pressure is 29.94 inches and rising." What does this mean? What are the units? We know the pressure of our car tires should be about 35. Again, what's the meaning and what are the units?

The pressure reported during weather reports is *barometric* pressure. It is the air pressure at that location, sometimes corrected to sea-level pressure. If your location is at or near sea level, there is no correction—the number given is the actual air pressure there. If your location is significantly higher than sea level, like Denver or Santa Fe, then the reported pressure has been corrected to the corresponding sea-level value. For example, sea-level pressure is about 30 inches, whereas Santa Fe pressure is about 24 inches. Travelers would become confused if they heard that the pressure at Santa Fe is 24 inches, so weather services correct the pressure by giving the corresponding sea-level pressure, about 30 inches, during weather reports. People like to know the barometric pressure because high pressure usually means fair weather while low pressure indicates stormy weather is on the way.

The unit of barometric pressure is inches of mercury. Mercury is a liquid metal that is quite dense (over 13 times the density of water). A filled glass tube of mercury about 30 inches high with a vacuum above the mercury column can be supported by sea-level air pressure. This instrument is a barometer and it can be conveniently used on a tabletop. So a barometric pressure of 29.94 inches means the air pressure can hold up a column of mercury 29.94 inches tall.

Why use mercury instead of a more common liquid like water? Because water is less dense than mercury, air pressure can hold up a much taller column of water. Air pressure can hold up a water column about 34 feet tall. This is taller than a three-story building. A 34-foot high barometer would not fit on most tabletops because ceilings are usually only 10-12 feet high. So a water barometer would not be a very convenient instrument to use. Consequently a mercury barometer is preferred, and it has become the standard.

The pressure in car tires is about 35 pounds per square inch (psi). One psi is not the same as one inch of mercury. These are different units of pressure. One psi is approximately the same pressure as two inches of mercury, so a tire inflation pressure is about 70 inches of mercury, but nobody ever uses this unit for tire inflation. Instead we routinely say "35 psi," and we mean that the air pressure inside the tire is 35 psi greater than the air pressure outside the tire. Note that what is important is the pressure difference between the air inside and outside the tire. The required pressure depends on the weight

sealed end
of tube
(vacuum)

height of
column

reservoir of
mercury

open end
of tube

of the loaded car and the area of tire in contact with the ground. When the load increases, the pressure must increase. When the contact area decreases, the tire pressure must increase. For example, the weight of a loaded bicycle is smaller than a loaded car, but the contact area of the tire is much smaller, so bicycle tires are inflated to higher pressure than car tires. Bicycle tires are usually inflated to 45 psi and higher.

What about other pressures we encounter daily? When we write with a pencil or ball point pen, we apply pressure to make the pencil or pen write with the desired darkness. Typically, the pressure applied to the writing surface is several hundred psi. This is the pressure at the tip of the pencil or pen, and it's applied to the paper surface. Unlike air pressure in a tire, we don't have to "contain" this pressure by confining the air and keeping it from leaking, as we do in a tire. For pencil or pen, we just apply the pressure at will and then release it when we're finished. In contrast, it's more difficult to maintain air pressure in a tire. In general, creating pressure in a gas is more difficult than a solid.

# Surface Tension

A water strider moves quickly across the surface of a pond. On wax paper, small drops of water bead up into tiny balls. When carefully placed in a pan of water, a paper clip floats even though steel is many times denser than water. All of these things happen because of an amazing phenomenon called *surface tension*.

Surface tension is a force acting in the surface of a liquid which makes the liquid act as if it is covered with a thin, stretchy "skin." Surface tension is caused by the attractive forces between the molecules in a liquid. This attractive force between like molecules is called *cohesion*. (The attraction between unlike molecules is called *adhesion*.)

Let's look at how cohesion produces surface tension. A glass of water contains a gigantic number of individual water molecules because these molecules are very tiny. Think of one of these tiny water molecules somewhere beneath the surface. It is being attracted (remember cohesion) in all directions by the other molecules surrounding it. These attractions pull the molecule equally in all directions and, as a result, the molecule moves in a random "dance" below the surface of the water.

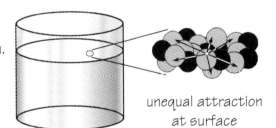

equal attraction
in all directions

Now consider a molecule at the surface of the water. This molecule is not free to move around randomly like the molecules below the surface. This is because it is not being attracted equally in all directions. The surface molecule is only being attracted to the sides (by other molecules in the surface) and down (by molecules below the surface). There are few water molecules in the air directly above the water to pull the surface molecule in that direction. This unbalanced situation, with the molecule being pulled to the sides and down, creates a tension that tries to pull it toward the center of the water. It is this tension in the surface molecules which makes the water act like it has a skin.

unequal attraction
at surface

All liquids have surface tension, but its strength varies greatly from liquid to liquid. Interestingly, it is especially strong in the most common liquid, water. Water has a surface tension which is much stronger than other liquids like oil or rubbing alcohol. You will witness the powerful surface tension of water in action when you do the activity *Pennies in a Cup*.

The surface tension of water changes dramatically when soap is added to the water. The surface tension of soapy water is less than half that of water. When liquid soap is added to the water, the soap molecules wedge themselves between the water molecules, weakening the hydrogen bonds. This effect decreases the surface tension at the air/water interface. With reduced surface tension, ripples form more easily, and they grow. This ripple growth is Rayleigh-Taylor Instability, and it causes the water to spill from the jar. This is demonstrated graphically in the activity *More Pennies in a Cup*.

An important effect of surface tension is that it makes the water surface smooth. The surface of a lake or pond appears glassy smooth on a windless day. Surface tension keeps ripples from forming and it smoothes out any ripples present. So surface tension is an effective tool for blocking Rayleigh-Taylor Instability, which depends on ripples to create the spilling of water.

As you do the experiments in this book, you will get to experience the amazing power of surface tension first hand. Have an enjoyable learning adventure.

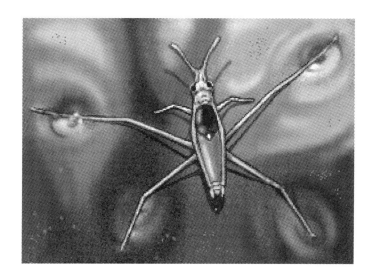

# Two Oceans

Astronauts viewing planet Earth observe that humans live at the boundary of two great expanses of fluids. At and above the land where people live is a huge expanse of air that we call the *atmosphere*. It covers 100% of the Earth's area. From an astronaut's perspective, people live near and atop oceans of seawater, like the Atlantic Ocean and Pacific Ocean, that cover over 70% of the Earth's area. If we call these water oceans *sea-oceans* and we call the atmosphere an *air-ocean*, then we can say we live at the boundary between *two oceans*. We live at the bottom of the air-ocean and at the top of the sea-ocean. The air-ocean contains interesting things like birds, clouds, and air currents; the sea-ocean contains other interesting things like fish, marine mammals, and ocean currents.

The air-ocean and sea-ocean have important similarities that are often ignored. They are both fluids. They both have currents that strongly affect weather and climate at the Earth's surface. Because of gravity, fluid pressure increases with depth in both oceans. Both oceans help keep the Earth's surface temperature fairly moderate and life-supporting. People put lots of waste and pollution into both oceans. We usually ignore the air-ocean because it's invisible and we ignore the sea-ocean because most people don't live within visable range and we only see its surface. Scientists study both oceans and do not yet know precisely how they work and how to predict when and how changes will occur. Yet the air-ocean and sea-ocean are vital to plant life and animal life. Both oceans nurture and protect life.

Water and air currents, moving fluids, are important in oceans, and they determine the climate and weather on our planet. Understanding currents scientifically requires understanding the effects of fluid pressure and density as well as changes in fluid pressure and density. A good way to learn about fluid pressure and density and the effects of their changes is in the classroom laboratory by doing experiments about fluid instabilities and Cartesian Divers! This is an unusual way to study Earth Science, but it is remarkably effective to learn the science of fluids that is helpful to understand important ocean and atmosphere phenomena. It's difficult for a student to do an experiment involving the ocean or atmosphere other than just making observations, but a student can easily try lots of experiments about instabilities and divers using the activities in this book.

Weather is affected by the temperature of large bodies of water. For example, warm water in the South Atlantic Ocean during the late summer and fall spawns hurricanes. Thermal currents in the Pacific are responsible for El Niño conditions. Atmosphere and ocean currents change, and small changes in currents can become large changes. One way to make small changes is fluid insta- bility. Fluid instabilities, such as the Rayleigh-Taylor Instability, can trigger flows that can grow into currents. Oceanographers and meteorologists study currents, not instabilities, so we don't hear about the importance of instabilities in weather.

# Betwixt and Between:

## Topic
Interfaces

## Key Question
How can we classify interfaces (boundaries) among solids, liquids, and gases?

## Focus
Students will observe the interfaces between various combinations of solids, liquids, and gases by studying a pictorial harbor scene, by looking around the classroom and school grounds, and/or by browsing magazines.

## Guiding Documents
*Project 2061 Benchmark*
- *The action of gravitational force on regions of different densities causes them to rise or fall—and such circulation, influenced by the rotation of the earth produces winds and ocean currents.*

*NRC Standards*
- *Objects have many observable properties, including size, weight, shape, color, temperature, and the ability to react with other substances. Those properties can be measured using tools, such as rulers, balances, and thermometers.*
- *Different kinds of questions suggest different kinds of scientific investigations. Some investigations involve observing and describing objects, organisms, or events; some involve collecting specimens; some involve experiments; some involve seeking more information; some involve discovery of new objects and phenomena; and some involve making models.*

## Science
Phsical science
   Interfaces
      solids, liquids, gases

## Integrated Process
Observing

## Materials
Student sheets
Magazines that can be cut up

## Background Information
In preparation for studying the behavior of interfaces between fluids (liquids and gases), students must sharpen their awareness of interfaces in general. This activity requires students to observe and label interfaces which they have all seen before but rarely noticed as interfaces. The goal is to develop awareness of what is on each side of a boundary (interface) between two materials. For example, the surface of a pond is the interface between water (liquid) below and air (gas) above.

Interfaces play an enormous role in science and in everyday life. Many chemical reactions occur at interfaces between the reactants. Friction at interfaces is important in keeping cars on the roadways and preventing us from slipping on sidewalks. Most sports involve some form of contact and that occurs at interfaces.

## Management
1. This activity is intended to make students more aware of interfaces in nature and in everyday living. An interface is where two different materials touch.
2. Students should work alone to find at least one example of each of the seven types of interfaces before working in a group to find other examples.
3. Note that there are two types of liquid/liquid interfaces: the "mix" type is where the two liquids in contact will soon mix. For example, adding milk to coffee briefly produces a milk/coffee interface, but these liquids soon mix together and the interface between them disappears. The "non-mix" interface is between liquids that do not mix with each other, like salad oil and vinegar. Even shaking them does not thoroughly mix them; it just produces globules of one liquid within another. An oil slick on water is another non-mix example.

This activity leads into activities with fluid interfaces where one of the fluids is water, so emphasize the observation of liquid/liquid and liquid/gas interfaces.

The seven types of interfaces are:
   solid/solid
   solid/liquid
   solid/gas
   liquid/liquid (with mixing)
   liquid/liquid (without mixing)
   liquid/gas
   gas/gas

## Procedure
1. Give each student a copy of the *Interface Classification Matrix* and *Interface Harbor*, and instruct them to write down one interface in the picture for each of the seven categories.
2. Organize the students in groups of two or three and instruct them to make additional entries.

## Discussion

1. What is an interface? Give examples.
2. What are some examples of each of the seven categories of interfaces? [solid/solid: tire on roadway; solid/liquid: boat on water; solid/gas: roadway over air; liquid/liquid (with mixing): drainage water over ocean; liquid/liquid (no mixing): oil slick on water, gas/liquid: air over water surface; gas/gas: cloud, vapor vented into air]

## Extension

Make a poster for each of the seven interfaces on which students can add more examples during a week. Students may glue or tape examples from magazines that may be cut up or draw examples or even write them. Encourage unusual interfaces.

# Interface Harbor

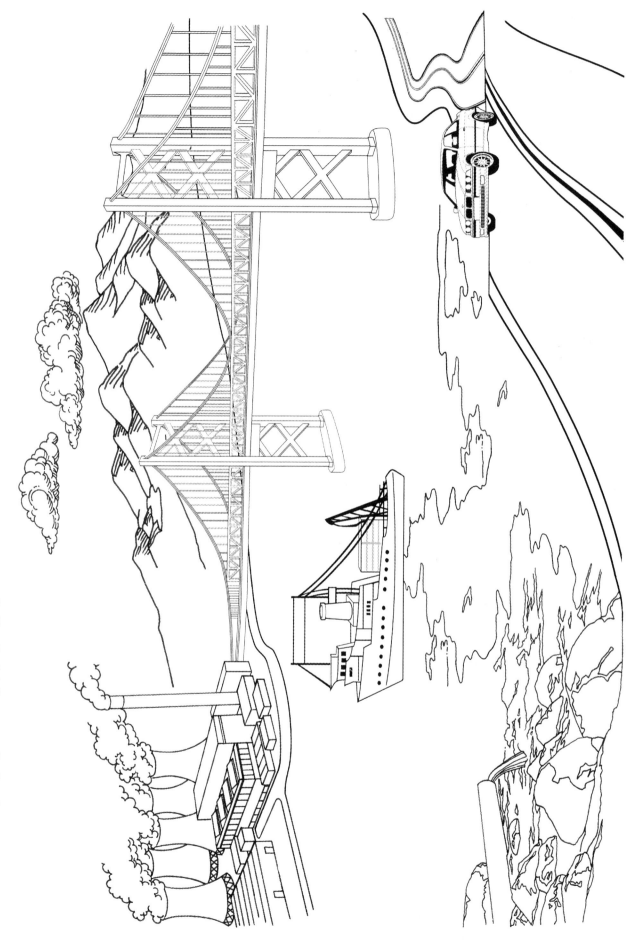

16

# Betwixt and Between: INTERFACE

## Classification Matrix

An interface is the boundary where two different materials touch. The materials may be solid, liquid, or gas. Inspect the *Interface Harbor* scene and think about the world around you. Then list interfaces of each type.

Solid/Solid: _____

_____

Solid/Liquid: _____

_____

Solid/Gas: _____

_____

Liquid/Liquid: _____

(mix) _____

_____

Liquid/Liquid: _____

(non-mix) _____

_____

Liquid/Gas: _____

_____

_____

Gas/Gas: _____

_____

## Topic
Spilling and mixing of fluids (Rayleigh-Taylor Instability)

## Key Question
How can water be held in an inverted container with various barriers?

## Focus
Students will learn the basic technique of controlling the Rayleigh-Taylor Instability that causes water to spill from an inverted baby food jar. They will use barriers having successively less strength and greater porosity: (1) index card, (2) facial tissue, (3) gauze or cheesecloth.

## Guiding Documents
*Project 2061 Benchmark*
• *The action of gravitational force on regions of different densities causes them to rise or fall—and such circulation, influenced by the rotation of the earth produces winds and ocean currents.*

*NCTM Standards 2000\**
• *Understand such attributes as length, area, weight, volume, and size of angle and select the appropriate type of unit for measuring each attribute*
• *Recognize and apply mathematics in contexts outside of mathematics*

## Math
Measurement
    area
    volume
    angle
Estimating

## Science
Physical science
    matter
        fluids (liquids and gases)
        Rayleigh-Taylor Instability

## Integrated Processes
Observing
Predicting
Comparing and contrasting
Inferring

## Materials
*For each group:*
    plastic tub for catching spilled water
    4-ounce baby food jar
    clear plastic drinking water or juice bottle, with label (approximately 500 mL)
    rubber bands
    index cards
    facial tissues
    5-inch squares of cheesecloth or gauze

## Background Information
Fill a clean baby food jar with water. Place an index card or laminated card over the mouth of the jar. Holding the card firmly on the jar, invert jar and card together. Release your hold on the index card and observe that the water does not spill out of the jar. This demonstration shows that air pressure below the card is sufficient to support the water within the jar. The card is held in place by the pressure balance of the water above the card and the air below, and by the slight adhesion of the card to the jar's rim.

What if the card is removed when the water jar is inverted? Then we have a water-above-air interface and we observe that the water spills out. Part of the reason for water spilling is gravity, but we know from experience with a card over the jar opening that air pressure is adequate to hold up the water in the jar. Something in addition to gravity must be happening to get the water spilling. That additional effect is called **Rayleigh-Taylor Instability** (RTI). The effect is that ripples at the water-over-air interface grow larger and larger because the higher-density fluid (water) is above the lower-density fluid (air). The water-above-air interface is an **unstable fluid interface**.

We can try to hold the water in the inverted jar by using barriers to keep ripples from forming at the water-over-air interface. The barriers will be permeable so the water is in contact with air, unlike the experiment with a card. However, students should first do the card-covered jar experiment to realize that air pressure is adequate to support the water. The barriers, tissue, and then gauze, are clearly too flimsy and porous to support the water held in the jar. The function of the barriers is to suppress formation of ripples and, remarkably, that's enough to hold the water. The following discussion reviews the pressure and density issues.

When the jar is upright, the water pressure at the surface is exactly equal to the air pressure. In the inverted jar, the pressure in the air pocket above the water is slightly reduced in order to equalize the water and air pressures at the lower water/air interface.

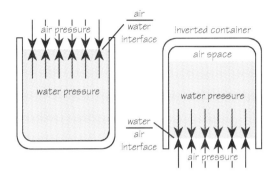

The density of water is about 800 times greater than the density of air. In the inverted jar, the higher-density water is on top of the lower-density air; therefore the water "spills" out of the jar. *When two fluids of different densities are in contact, and the higher density fluid is on top, ripples at the interface grow and grow and grow. That is the Rayleigh-Taylor Instability: the growth of ripples.* What we observe as spilling is the catastrophically large growth of ripples at the air/water interface.

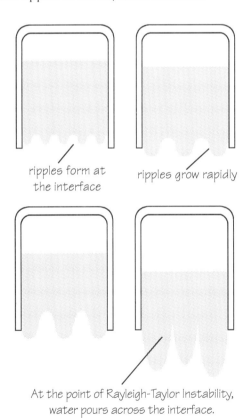

ripples form at the interface

ripples grow rapidly

At the point of Rayleigh-Taylor Instability, water pours across the interface.

In this activity students will explore three different methods of controlling ripple growth at the interface and therefore control spilling.

## Management
1. Organize your students into groups of two or three.
2. Have plastic tubs available to catch water spills. If weather permits, *Look Out Below!* is a great outdoor activity.
3. Have a good supply of paper towels or sponges on hand to absorb spills.
4. Provide extra index cards, facial tissues, and gauze squares.
5. Schedule at least 15 minutes for the estimation activity (the first student sheet) and 15 minutes to test each of the three barriers.
6. Demonstrate the basic technique of placing a barrier over the mouth of the jar, holding the barrier with one hand and inverting the jar with the other hand. **Do not have any water in the jar** when you demonstrate this technique. A student's hand may be too small to support the tissue or gauze barrier. In this instance, the index card can be used to support weaker barriers during the inversion process. If there is a problem with the index card sticking to the tissue or gauze, use a plastic playing card or laminated index card.
7. Review area (square cm) and volume (mL) measurement.
8. Save clear plastic water or juice bottles. Check each bottle to be sure its volume appears on the label.

## Procedure
1. Distribute the first student sheet.
2. Instruct the students to estimate the area of the open end of their jars by tracing around the open ends on the centimeter grid.
3. Have the students use their clear plastic water or juice bottle to determine an estimated volume of their baby food jars.
4. Assist students in making and recording these estimates.
5. Ask the *Key Question* and distribute the second student sheet.

*For the index card barrier:*
6. Instruct the students to record their prediction for the index card on their student sheets. Tell them to test their predictions and record their observations on their sheets. Help them to correctly draw the side view of the "barrier" before and after inverting their jars.

*For the facial tissue barrier:*
7. Assist the students in correctly placing the facial tissue over the mouth of the jar. Smooth the barrier to remove any wrinkles before inverting. Ask them to again record their predictions, invert their jars, and then record their observations on their sheets.

*For the gauze or cheesecloth barrier:*

8. To focus on the fact that the gauze or cheesecloth is porous (full of holes) tell the students to place the gauze over the mouth of an **empty** jar and to secure it with a rubber band. Then pour water into the jar **through** the gauze or cheesecloth. Smooth the barrier to remove any wrinkles before inverting.

9. Have the students once more record their predictions, invert their jars, and then record their observations.

## Discussion

*For the estimates of area and volume:*

1. What estimates did your group determine for both the area and volume measures? (Write these on the chalkboard.) Compare these estimates.

2. What explanations can you think of that would account for any differences in the measurements?

*For the index card:*

1. Were you surprised that the index card held the water in the jar?

2. Why do you think the index card held the water in the jar? (Listen for key words and phrases such as *pressure, force, air, surface tension,* etc.)

3. What did you observe about the shape of the barrier? (Organize the responses by using a tally method.)

Shape of Barrier

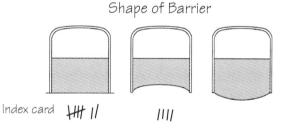

Index card   卌 ||          ||||

tissue

gauze

*For the facial tissue:*

1. How many of you predicted that the facial tissue barrier would contain the water in the jar?

2. What were your reasons for making that prediction?

3. Discuss the relative "strengths" between the index card and the facial tissue.

*For the gauze or cheesecloth:*

1. How many predicted the gauze or cheesecloth barrier would contain the water in the jar? Why?

## Extensions

1. Have the students make a chart to compare and contrast the three barriers.

| Sample Comparison Chart | | | |
|---|---|---|---|
| Property | Index card | Facial tissue | Gauze or cheesecloth |
| Strength Curvature Holes ___ ___ ___ | | | |

2. Have students make a *Critical Angle Protractor* (see the third student page) and measure the critical angle for each of the barriers (index card, tissue, and gauze). The *critical angle* is the tilt angle when water begins to leak out, either as a steady stream of drops or as a stream.

3. The gauze or cheese cloth proves that it's possible for a barrier to have holes. Could one or more holes be made in the index card and tissue barriers?

4. Test a variety of containers and sizes such as paper cups, plastic cups, wide-mouth bottles, and narrow-mouth bottles.

5. If students want to try these experiments with the clear plastic bottle used to estimate volumes, then they can change the pressure at the water-over-air interface by squeezing the inverted bottle of water. This is a different process of causing the water to fall than is Rayleigh-Taylor Instability. RTI requires first having a balance of pressures, which is easier to do in a glass bottle than a plastic bottle, so keeping water in an inverted plastic bottle is more difficult than in an inverted glass bottle.

6. Students may want to explore the limits of keeping water from spilling in inverted bottles with and without barriers. That is the subject of the *Trickle Triathlon* activity.

\* Reprinted with permission from *Principles and Standards for School Mathematics*, 2000 by the National Council of Teachers of Mathematics. All rights reserved.

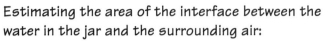

# LOOK OUT BELOW !

**Estimating the area of the interface between the water in the jar and the surrounding air:**

1. Invert your jar and place it on the grid.

2. Use your pencil and outline the open end of your jar.

3. Estimate the area of the outline by counting whole squares and parts of squares.

   The area is approximately

   _____ square cm

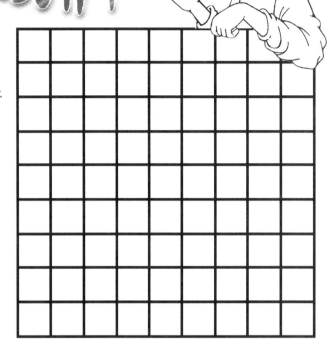

**Estimating the volume of the jar used in this activity:**

1. Examine the label on the clear plastic drinking water or juice bottle. Record the volume of the bottle that is printed on the label.

2. Fill the bottle with water.

3. Pour the water from the bottle into your jar until the jar is full.

4. Estimate the volume of the jar.

5. Record the estimated volume on the illustration of the jar.

Clear plastic drinking water or juice bottle

_____
volume in mL

volume in mL

# Look Out Below!

## index card

Predict whether or not the index card will contain the water when the jar is inverted:

*Observation*

Draw the shape of the barrier.

before jar is inverted

after jar is inverted

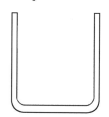

## facial tissue

Predict whether or not the facial tissue will contain the water when the jar is inverted.

*Observation*

Draw the shape of the barrier.

before jar is inverted

after jar is inverted

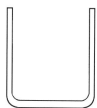

## gauze or cheesecloth

Predict whether or not the gauze or cheesecloth will contain the water when the jar is inverted.

*Observation*

Draw the shape of the barrier.

before jar is inverted

after jar is inverted

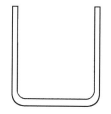

# Critical Angle Protractor

**Construction:**

1. Copy or print this page on card stock or glue it to a piece of cardboard.
2. Cut out the Protractor piece, and the Movable Arm.
3. Use a paper punch to put a hole in the Movable Arm.
4. Use a paper punch to make a pivot hole in each piece.
5. Attach the Movable Arm to the top of the Protractor with a paper fastener.

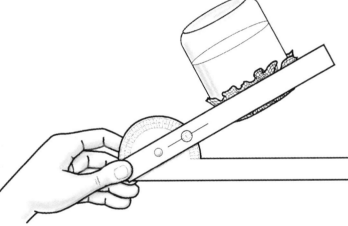

**Using the Critical Angle Protractor:**

1. Hold the Protractor in one hand as shown in the diagram. Rest the bottom arm on the edge of the plastic tub used to catch water spills.
2. As the student holding the inverted jar slowly turns the jar, adjust the Movable Arm so that its lower edge remains parallel to the mouth of the jar.
3. Read the angle on the Protractor scale through the hole on the Movable Arm.
4. The angle at which Rayleigh-Taylor Instability occurs is called the critical angle.

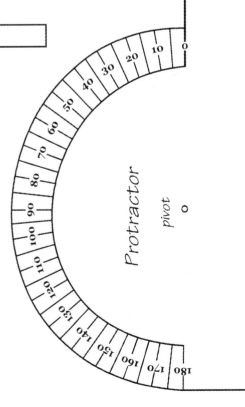

© 2001 AIMS Education Foundation

# Sauces
## A commercial application of blocking Rayleigh-Taylor Instability

Rayleigh-Taylor Instability (RTI) is involved in the pouring of some, but not all, sauces and other foods that can sometimes be stubborn about flowing. For example, RTI influences the pouring of soy sauce and some hot pepper sauces, but not ketchup or yogurt.

When I try to pour some soy sauce on my food, I turn the bottle upside down and a few drops come out, that's all. I look closely at the opening of the soy sauce bottle and observe that it's only a few millimeters in diameter and that another drop is poised to come out, but it seems stuck. The drop's surface is the interface between soy sauce above and air below. The surface is a fluid interface with the higher-density fluid (soy sauce) above the lower-density fluid (air). Because the higher-density fluid is on top, Rayleigh-Taylor Instability should occur, causing the soy sauce to pour out. But the drop doesn't pour.

The "bottle engineers" designed the opening of the soy sauce bottle to block Rayleigh-Taylor Instability! The opening size of a few millimeters inside diameter is "matched" to the surface tension of the soy sauce so Rayleigh-Taylor Instability is blocked. The surface tension of the soy sauce is great enough to smooth small ripples on the drop wanting to exit, so the drop stays put. Do the bottle engineers know about Rayleigh-Taylor Instability? Probably not by name, but they certainly know about the effect. They design the opening to produce a fluid interface with the higher-density fluid on top.

How do I get more soy sauce out? I need to make ripples that are too large for surface tension to smooth, so Rayleigh-Taylor Instability happens. I can make these large ripples by shaking the bottle or by hitting it. Another way is to tilt it. I could even blow air toward the stubborn drop, but that's generally not socially acceptable. Any of these methods produce ripples adequate to trigger Rayleigh-Taylor Instability and thereby get the liquid pouring, at least for a spurt or two.

Hot pepper sauces and some flavorings use the same principle of blocking Rayleigh-Taylor Instability. The opening size of the bottle is matched to the surface tension of the liquid so only a drop or two spills out before I need to shake it to produce ripples large enough to start the pouring.

Knowing that Rayleigh-Taylor Instability is involved in the pouring of soy sauce, hot pepper sauce, and other flavorings, I might expect that the reluctance of ketchup and yogurt to pour out is also related to Rayleigh-Taylor Instability. Alas, this is NOT the case! The pouring (or lack of it!) of ketchup and yogurt is governed by a different effect. Rayleigh-Taylor Instability applies to ordinary fluids, meaning liquids and gases, that are always capable of flowing.

Ketchup and yogurt are not ordinary liquids. They are called "thixotropic fluids" (pronounced thick-seh-trah-pick). They sometimes behave as solids and sometimes as liquids. Another thixotropic fluid is mayonnaise. In contrast, Rayleigh-Taylor Instability doesn't apply to solids because solids cannot have ripples at interfaces that are capable of growing like ripples on a liquid surface. Ketchup and yogurt don't flow initially because their particles form a structure that causes solid-like behavior. I must apply enough stresses to break up these structures in order to produce liquid-like flows. I apply such stresses by vigorously shaking the container or by stirring with a utensil. The thixotropic property is a condition of the bulk material in ketchup and yogurt, whereas Rayleigh-Taylor Instability occurs at a surface or interface.

# TRICKLE TRIATHLON

## Topic
The spilling of fluids (Rayleigh-Taylor Instability)

## Key Questions
Event # 1
*Look!, Mom, No Barrier!*
What is the largest opening area of an inverted, water-filled container that can be supported by air without the use of a barrier at the water-over-air interface?

Event #2
*Amazing Tissue*
What is the largest, tissue-covered opening of an inverted, water-filled container?

Event #3
*Movable Mesh*
What is the minimum number of threads of a cheesecloth mesh needed to contain water in an inverted juice bottle?

## Focus
Small groups of students will explore the limitations of controlling Rayleigh-Taylor Instability (RTI) by competing in a three-event "Olympics." The goal of each event is for students to develop techniques to confine water in an inverted bottle and to find the limit of how well their technique works. Students will also assess how sturdy ("robustness" on a stability scale) the water-over-air interface is for each test.

*Look!, Mom, No Barrier! (Event #1):*
The students will experiment with a variety of water-filled containers to determine the largest opening that still keeps the water in when no barrier is used.

*Amazing Tissue (Event #2):*
The students will develop techniques to keep water within an inverted, water-filled container using a single-ply tissue to cover the jar opening (at the water-over-air interface), and they will test increasingly larger jar openings to determine the maximum opening that can contain the water.

*Movable Mesh (Event #3):*
The students will develop methods for changing the pattern of cheesecloth threads to confine water in an inverted juice bottle, and they will determine the most open pattern of threads (i.e., the pattern with fewest threads) that will keep the water in.

## Guiding Documents
*Project 2061 Benchmark*
* *The action of gravitational force on regions of different densities causes them to rise or fall—and such circulation, influenced by the rotation of the earth produces winds and ocean currents.*

*NRC Standards*
* *Objects have many observable properties, including size, weight, shape, color, temperature, and the ability to react with other substances. Those properties can be measured using tools, such as rulers, balances, and thermometers.*
* *Different kinds of questions suggest different kinds of scientific investigations. Some investigations involve observing and describing objects, organisms, or events; some involve collecting specimens; some involve experiments; some involve seeking more information; some involve discovery of new objects and phenomena; and some involve making models.*

*NCTM Standards 2000\**
* *Understand such attributes as length, area, weight, volume, and size of angle and select the appropriate type of unit for measuring each attribute*
* *Recognize and apply mathematics in contexts outside of mathematics*

## Science
Physical science
    matter
        fluids (liquids and gases)
            Rayleigh-Taylor Instability

## Integrated Processes
Observing
Comparing and contrasting

Collecting and recording data
Interpreting data
Applying

## Materials
- Smooth cards, index cards, laminated cards or other flat surfaces (used to support water/air interface while inverting the bottle)
- Sponges, bowls to catch spills and clean up

*Look, Mom, No Barrier! (Event #1):*
- Assortment of straws, jars, bottles, test tubes or other cylindrical containers having opening diameter in the range 5-15 mm
- Index cards
- Hole punches, preferably different sizes, or scissors for cutting holes in index cards. The holes range 5-15 mm diameter.

*Amazing Tissue (Event #2):*
- Assortment of jars, bottles, or other cylindrical containers, like hard-plastic leftover containers, having opening diameter in the range 2.5-15 cm (1-6 inches). Encourage students to bring some from home. Glass and hard-plastic containers are preferred. Containers that can be easily distorted with hand-pressure should not be used.
- Name-brand facial tissue
- Rubber bands

*Movable Mesh (Event #3):*
- Identical, glass, juice bottles, one for each group. Glass, 16-oz. juice bottles which have 20-mm diameter openings work well. Glass soda bottles may be substituted.
- Cheesecloth
- Scissors
- Sharpened pencil or toothpick
- Rubber bands

## Background Information
When a water-filled bottle is turned upside down, the water will easily pour out if the bottle opening is sufficiently large. Sometimes it pours smoothly while other times it pours roughly, making a "glug-glug-glug" sound. The water pours out because ripples quickly form at the water-over-air interface and then RTI causes the ripples to grow rapidly into the stream or "glugs" of pouring water.

When a liquid-filled bottle with an opening only a few millimeters in diameter is turned upside down, most of the liquid stays in the bottle. For example, inverting a bottle of soy sauce usually causes only a few drops to pour out. Similarly, filling a clean, sample-size, mouthwash bottle with water and then turning it upside down will usually produce only a few drops of spilled water. Most of the liquid stays in the

inverted bottles because surface tension smooths the water-over-air interface so that RTI is blocked. The water pressure equals the air pressure at the water-over-air interface so no force is trying to push the water out. Controlling the RTI keeps the water within the bottles.

This effect is similar to confining water within a drinking straw (usually 4-6 mm diameter) by dipping the straw into a glass of water, covering the top of the straw with your finger, and lifting the straw from the water.

When your finger seals the top of the straw, the combination of air and water pressure in the straw equals the air pressure below the straw. So the pressure above the water-over-air interface equals the pressure below the interface and there is no unbalanced pressure trying to expel the water. RTI is blocked because surface tension smooths the water-over-air interface, and the water stays in the straw. When your finger is removed, the air pressure within the straw increases so the combination of air pressure and water pressure in the straw exceeds the air pressure just below the water-over-air interface. This pressure imbalance causes the water to spurt out.

*Look, Mom, No Barrier! (Event #1):*
A water-over-air interface of about 5 mm diameter or less can easily be stabilized without the use of a barrier. How much larger diameter can a water-over-air interface be self-supporting in this manner? For example, can water be confined in an inverted test tube, typically 12-15 mm diameter, without a barrier? This activity determines the largest area of water-over-air interface without a barrier and develops methods needed to maximize this area.

*Amazing Tissue (Event #2):*
Water can be contained within an inverted bottle by using a tissue to cover the opening. The tissue aids surface tension of the water to keep the water-tissue-air interface smooth so no ripples form. This process

controls the RTI that would otherwise cause the water to pour out. The combination of surface tension and strength of the wet tissue makes the water-tissue-air interface taut, smooth, and ripple-free.

*Movable Mesh (Event #3):*

The opening of a soda or juice bottle (typically 20 mm in diameter) is too large for surface tension alone to keep water in the inverted bottle. However, by carefully covering the bottle opening with a piece of cheesecloth, the water-over-air interface can be smoothed enough to keep the water in when the bottle is inverted. The challenge is to move threads in cheesecloth to create an increasingly open pattern that still confines the water when the bottle is inverted. A series of tests with fewer threads each test is needed to find the limit.

## Management

1. Organize students into groups of three to six.
2. Have containers and sponges available to catch water spills.
3. Encourage students to bring containers from home. Glass jars, bottles, and hard plastic containers are preferred over plastic ones because plastic ones can be distorted by squeezing, which affects the water-over-air interfaces.
4. Be sure the jars and bottles are clean so that no residue in the bottle changes the surface tension of the water.
5. For *Event #2, Amazing Tissue*, use the same brand of tissue for all groups.
6. Weather permitting, this investigation can be done outdoors to minimize cleanup of spilled water and to encourage students to push the limits of bottle-opening diameter for confining water.
7. An alternative to the Olympic-style format is to have one to two groups do each event and report results back to the entire class.

## Procedure

1. For each event in sequence, have the students predict the result and record the prediction on the student sheet.
2. Once a water-filled bottle is ready for a test, the student should cover the bottle opening with a hand or an index card or some other flat surface while inverting the bottle. After the bottle is inverted, have them wait several seconds for any sloshing to stop, then carefully remove the flat surface to see whether the water will stay within the inverted bottle. Students must develop skill in removing the flat surface gently. It's okay if some water drips out when the flat surface is first removed. After the dripping stops, the water must not drip, stream, or gush out for five seconds for the test to count as a successful event.

3. Direct the students to gently shake the inverted bottle or straw each time to see how much vibration is needed to cause drops of water to spill out and rate the "robustness."
4. Have them record the observations and compare with their predictions.
5. Offer "gold, silver, bronze medals" or other suitable awards for the groups having the largest openings (*Events #1* and *#2*) and fewest threads (*Event #3*) that hold the water in. The medalist team must demonstrate their winning entry to the entire class.

*Look, Mom, No Barrier! (Event #1):*

1. Have students use their finger to hold water in a straw (see *Background Information*).
2. Next, have them use a bottle with a small diameter like Tabasco™ sauce, soy sauce, sample-size or travel-size bottle of mouthwash or shampoo. Direct them to invert the water-filled container and observe whether the water stays in after a few drops drip out.
3. Urge groups to test bottles with openings that are 5-15 mm (about $\frac{1}{4}$- to $\frac{3}{4}$-inch) in diameter. Test tubes and "culture tubes" from chemical supplies are also useful. Make certain that students observe that bottle shape is unimportant but the diameter opening is very important in keeping water in the inverted container.
4. Another method is to use a perforated index card as a barrier for keeping water within an inverted baby-food jar or juice bottle. Direct students to make a single, clean hole in the index card and measure its hole diameter. Fill the jar with water, cover the opening with the perforated card, turn the jar upside-down and observe whether the water stays in. It may help if they cover the hole while the container is being inverted. If the water stays in the bottle, have them do another test with a larger hole to determine the largest hole that contains the water without use of a barrier. Inform students that if the water does not drip, stream, or gush out for five seconds, it counts as a successful event.
5. For each test have them observe and record whether the water stays confined and the robustness of the interface.

*Amazing Tissue (Event #2):*

1. Direct students to use a *single-ply* tissue to cover the opening of a water-filled bottle. Most tissues are two-ply so students should separate them first and use only one layer.
2. Have them secure the tissue with a rubber band around the mouth of the bottle. (This is not required, but it simplifies the process of inverting the jar.)
3. Instruct them to use a flat surface to support the tissue while inverting the bottle. Have them

carefully remove the supporting flat surface to see whether the water-over-air interface will keep the water confined in the bottle. As students become more skillful, use of the supporting surface becomes optional.

4. Have students observe and record whether the water stays confined and the robustness of the interface.

5. Urge them to try water-filled containers with increasingly larger openings. This requires more care in forming the wet tissue on the water surface and supporting the tissue while inverting the jar. Have them determine the largest opening for which a single-ply tissue confines the water when the container is upside down.

*Movable Mesh (Event #3):*
1. Each group should use the same type of bottle. Standard glass juice and soda bottles work well.

2. Have the students cover the water-filled bottle opening with a piece of cheesecloth, secured to the bottle opening with a rubber band. For each test, the student will use a sharpened pencil or toothpick to move the cheesecloth threads into a more open pattern and then test it to see whether the water stays in and how robust is the interface. The goal of later tests is to have fewer threads in contact with the water surface but still have the water stay in the inverted bottle.

3. As done in *Events #1* and *#2*, have them use a flat surface like a hand, index card, or laminated card to support the water over air interface while turning the bottle over.

4. For each test have students observe and record whether the water stays confined and the robustness of the interface using the stability scale on the student page.

## Discussion
*Look, Mom, No Barrier! (Event #1):*
1. What techniques helped you increase the area of the self-supporting water-over-air interface? What is necessary to make still larger self-supporting interfaces? [e.g., a steadier way to hold the container, a better method for inverting it, or more time after it's inverted before removing the supporting flat surface]

2. Why do you think certain liquid containers (Tabasco™ sauce, soy sauce) are designed with narrow openings while others (soda bottles) have larger openings? How does the opening size relate to the purpose of the bottle?

*Amazing Tissue (Event #2):*
1. What techniques helped you increase the area of the tissue-supported water/air interface? What is necessary to make still larger tissue-supported interfaces?

2. What limits how large a tissue-covered opening can support the water in an inverted container?

3. What have you learned about the design of tissues?

*Movable Mesh (Event #3):*
1. What configuration and number of cheesecloth threads just barely kept the water in?

2. For this configuration, estimate the greatest open area without threads. That is, estimate or measure the largest rectangular area bordered by threads. How does this area compare with the results in *Event #1*?

## Extensions
*Look, Mom, No Barrier! (Event #1):*
1. Repeat the investigations with soapy water and notice that the hole diameter must now be smaller.

2. Test other liquids.

3. Try other shapes of the hole (square, triangular).

*Amazing Tissue (Event #2):*
1. Try other brands of tissue and two-ply tissue.

2. Try samples of other paper designed to get wet, like toilet paper and paper towels.

*Movable Mesh (Event #3):*
1. Move the cheesecloth threads to form shapes other than a grid (e.g., wagon-wheel spokes, parallel threads) to test whether those configurations are more effective than the rectangular grid.

\* Reprinted with permission from *Principles and Standards for School Mathematics,* 2000 by the National Council of Teachers of Mathematics. All rights reserved.

# TRICKLE TRIATHLON

## FIRST EVENT
## LOOK, MOM, NO BARRIER!

### Instructions

1. Use a clean bottle with a small opening like a soy sauce bottle or a sample-size mouthwash bottle.
2. Use the Inside Diameter Gauges to measure and record the inside diameter of the opening. (See instructions below.)
3. Fill the bottle with water.
4. Carefully invert the water-filled container and observe whether the water stays in after a few drops drip out.
5. Record the "stability" rating.

Prediction: Maximum diameter opening = _____ mm

| Diameter of Opening (mm) | Type of Container | Stability Rating |
|---|---|---|
|  |  |  |

### Stability Rating

| | |
|---|---|
| 1 | any little motion causes water to **stream** out |
| 2 | any little motion causes water to **drip** out |
| 3 | stays, even with a **little** shaking |
| 4 | stays, even with **moderate** shaking |
| 5 | robust, like a drinking straw |

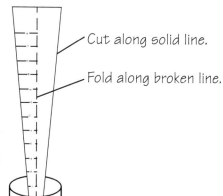

Cut along solid line.

Fold along broken line.

### Instructions for Cutting Out and Folding the Inside Diameter Gauges

Cut along the outside edge of both the long and short Inside Diameter Gauge. Fold each gauge along the broken line. Insert the narrow end of the gauge into the opening of the bottle.

# TRICKLE TRIATHLON

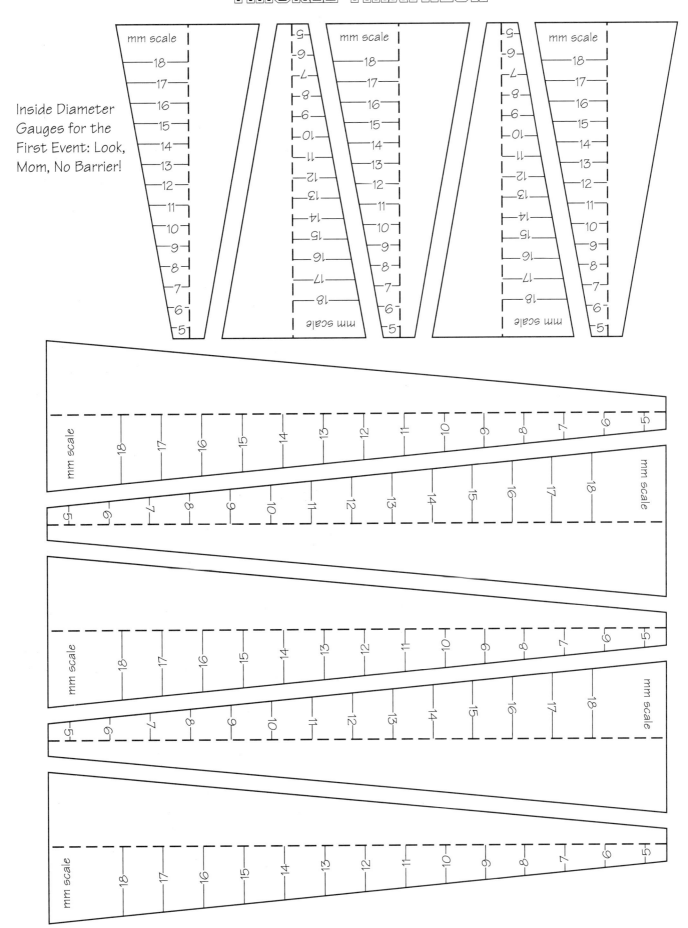

Inside Diameter Gauges for the First Event: Look, Mom, No Barrier!

# TRICKLE TRIATHLON

## SECOND EVENT
## AMAZING TISSUE

### Stability Rating

| | |
|---|---|
| 1 | any little motion causes water to **stream** out |
| 2 | any little motion causes water to **drip** out |
| 3 | stays, even with a **little** shaking |
| 4 | stays, even with **moderate** shaking |
| 5 | robust, like a drinking straw |

### Instructions

1. Use the Inside Diameter Gauge to measure the opening.
2. Use a single-ply tissue to cover the opening of a water-filled bottle. If your tissue is two-ply, separate it first and use only one layer.
3. Secure the tissue with a rubber band around the mouth of the bottle. (This is not required, but it simplifies the process of inverting the jar.)
4. Use a flat surface to support the tissue while inverting the bottle. Carefully remove the supporting flat surface to see whether the water-over-air interface will keep the water confined in the bottle.
5. Observe and record whether the water stays confined and identify and record the robustness of the interface (The Stability Rating).

| Diameter of Opening (mm) | Container Material (glass, firm plastic, squeezable plastic, etc.) | Stability Rating |
|---|---|---|
| | | |
| | | |
| | | |
| | | |
| | | |
| | | |

# TRICKLE TRIATHLON

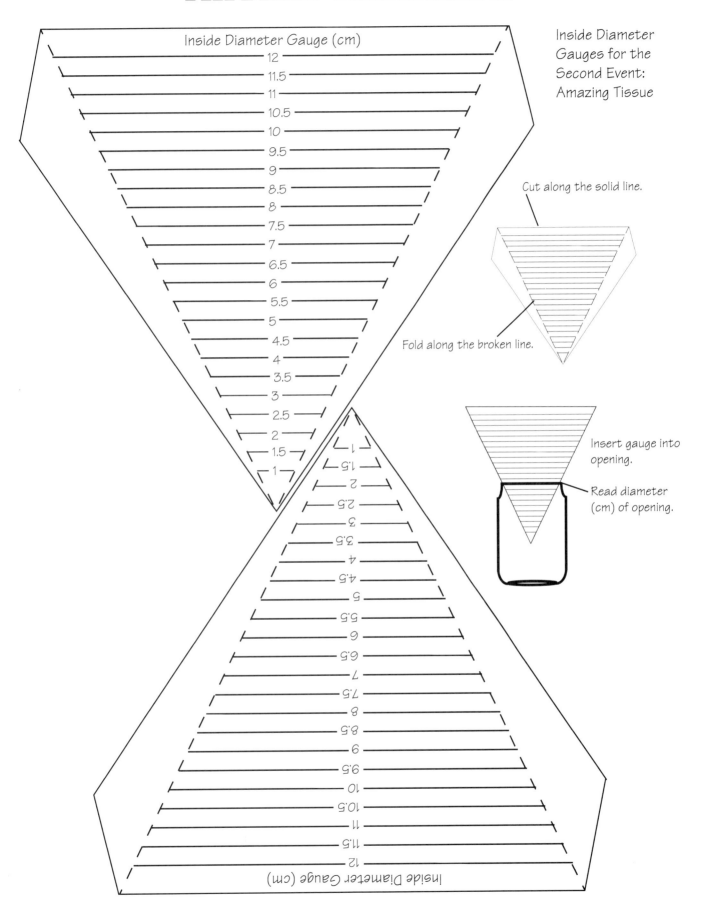

Inside Diameter Gauge (cm)

12
11.5
11
10.5
10
9.5
9
8.5
8
7.5
7
6.5
6
5.5
5
4.5
4
3.5
3
2.5
2
1.5
1

Inside Diameter Gauges for the Second Event: Amazing Tissue

Cut along the solid line.

Fold along the broken line.

Insert gauge into opening.

Read diameter (cm) of opening.

1
1.5
2
2.5
3
3.5
4
4.5
5
5.5
6
6.5
7
7.5
8
8.5
9
9.5
10
10.5
11
11.5
12

Inside Diameter Gauge (cm)

SPILLS AND RIPPLES

33

© 2001 AIMS Education Foundation

# TRICKLE TRIATHLON

## THIRD EVENT
## MOVABLE MESH

Use the point of a pencil to move and straighten the threads of the cheesecloth.

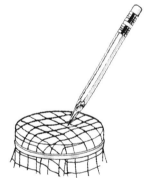

Move individual threads to the side of the opening to make a rectangular grid of threads.

Prediction: Minimum number of threads to contain water = _____

a 6 x 5 grid of threads

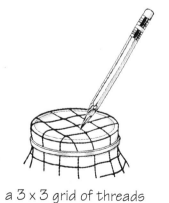

a 3 x 3 grid of threads

34

# TRICKLE TRIATHLON

Name _____

| Number of Threads | Shape of Thread Array | Stability Rating |
|---|---|---|
| 6 x 6 | | |
| | | |
| | | |
| | | |
| | | |
| | | |
| | | |
| | | |
| | | |
| | | |

### Stability Rating

| | | |
|---|---|---|
| 1 | — | any little motion causes water to **stream** out |
| 2 | — | any little motion causes water to **drip** out |
| 3 | — | stays, even with a **little** shaking |
| 4 | — | stays, even with **moderate** shaking |
| 5 | — | robust, like a drinking straw |

### Instructions

1. Move the cheesecloth threads to make the grid more open.
2. Count and record the number of threads in each direction.
3. Use a flat surface on the bottle's opening and carefully invert the bottle.
4. Check if water stays in the bottle. Determine and record the "stability" rating.

# Flow Fingers

## Topic
Flow patterns of mixing liquids

## Key Question
What flow patterns are observed when a drop of food coloring falls through still water?

## Focus
Students will observe both the simplicity and complexity of flow patterns produced by a drop of food coloring falling through still water.

## Guiding Documents
*Project 2061 Benchmark*
- *The action of gravitational force on regions of different densities causes them to rise or fall—and such circulation, influenced by the rotation of the earth produces winds and ocean currents.*

*NRC Standard*
- *Develop descriptions, explanations, predictions, and models using evidence.*

## Math
Geometry and spatial sense
Measurement
    length
    time

## Science
Physical science
    liquid flow

## Integrated Processes
Observing
Predicting
Collecting and recording data

## Materials
*For each group:*
    one or more tall, clear containers of water (Useful inexpensive containers include: tennis-ball container made of clear plastic with the label removed (available free at tennis courts), clear two-liter bottles with the label removed, and wide-mouth glass jars)
    food coloring, several colors
    eyedropper
    stopwatch or clock with second hand
Optional: still camera and/or video camera

## Background Information
A water/air interface is an interface between two fluids where the higher-density fluid (water) is a liquid and the lower-density fluid (air) is a gas. This *liquid/gas interface* is extremely familiar to us. The surface of a pond, a glass of water, or the ocean are common examples. A water/air interface is "Rayleigh-Taylor unstable" when the high-density fluid (water) is above the lower-density fluid (air). Ripples at the water-over-air interface grow *rapidly* because the densities are markedly different, water density being about 800 times greater than air density.

*Liquid/liquid interfaces* are also unstable when the higher-density liquid is on top. For example, the density of food coloring is greater than the density of water. Food coloring above water creates a Rayleigh-Taylor unstable interface. However, the densities of food coloring and water are close, so the ripples at the interface grow more slowly. The flow patterns created by the interfacial instability are more easily observed when the ripples grow slowly. Flow patterns produce a signature of the instability. For example, Rayleigh-Taylor Instability creates a *spike* of the higher-density fluid penetrating into the lower-density fluid, and a *bubble* of the lower-density fluid protruding into the higher-density fluid. Water being poured is actually a Rayleigh-Taylor spike, and air bubbling up through an inverted bottle that is quickly being emptied of liquid creates Rayleigh-Taylor bubbles.

Observing the Rayleigh-Taylor Instability of food coloring and water enables the student to discover other characteristics of this flow pattern. Also, the student may observe some of the beauty and wonder of fluid dynamics. These flows appear complicated, but they are composed of only a few basic shapes. These basic shapes occur again and again during the same flow. More advanced studies of these flows have been used to investigate the scientific distinction between order and chaos.

The following sequence of drawings is typical of what will be seen when a drop of food coloring is placed in still water.

As the drop enters the water, it generally forms a ring. The ring is caused by the drop passing through the water surface. It is a "vortex ring," the same effect as a "smoke ring." Sometimes the drop extends from the interface down into the

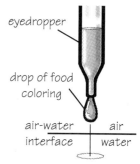

eyedropper

drop of food coloring

air-water interface    air

                water

water as a thin line of food coloring before turning into a ring.

As the ring moves downward, it expands and becomes wavy in form. This waviness of a vortex ring is called the "Widnall Instability," after Prof. Sheila Widnall, who discovered it in the 1970s.

Sections of the wavy ring, still moving downward, extend into leg-shaped loops having the appearance of tentacles. These tentacles are *Rayleigh-Taylor spikes.*

Foot pads form at the bottom of the loops. These appear as mushroom caps that have been turned upside down.

The loops lengthen and often additional loops spring from the foot pads.

## Management

The water containers should be filled at least ten minutes before the addition of food coloring. It is essential that the water be as still as possible. The containers should be placed on sturdy tables, away from any vibrations or air currents.

## Procedure

1. Have each student predict (i.e., guess) what the shape of a food-coloring drop falling through still water will be. Will it remain a drop until it hits the bottom of the water container? Will it diffuse and promptly fill the container with a pale hue of that color? Each student's guess may be narrative or sketched.

2. Direct the students to use the eyedropper to release a drop of food color about 1 cm above the water surface. Have them record the number and shape of the major features: ring, thin tentacles, inverted mushroom-shaped caps. Have them measure and record the distance of the shape from the water's surface.

3. Ask the students to determine how long they can see features like the initial ring, the tentacles, and the mushroom caps.

4. Have them measure the time from when the food coloring drop enters the water until the coloring reaches the bottom of the container. Also have them measure the time for the water to become uniformly colored.

5. Urge the students to repeat these steps several times.

6. If a still camera is available, have students take photographs for doing more detailed analysis later. (These photos may be suitable holiday gifts for parents or school fund-raisers.) A video could also be made.

## Discussion

1. What features of the flow pattern are reproducible? What features vary a lot? If you try very hard to make two flow patterns look exactly the same by starting the drop in exactly the same way, how well can you do?

2. If a student were absent, how would you describe the results to this student when he/she returned to school? Use oral presentations, hand gestures, and drawings to describe the flows. [Vocabulary words to embed in the above narrative: inverted mushroom, ring, tentacles.]

## Extensions

1. Repeat the procedure soon after filling the bottle, before the water has become still. Notice the dramatic changes to the flow patterns caused by the water currents.

2. Release the drop of food coloring from different heights above the water surface and observe differences of flow.

3. Release drops of different colors sequentially and notice the places where they overlap. Do two colors pass through each other or do they mix into a third color?

# Flow Fingers

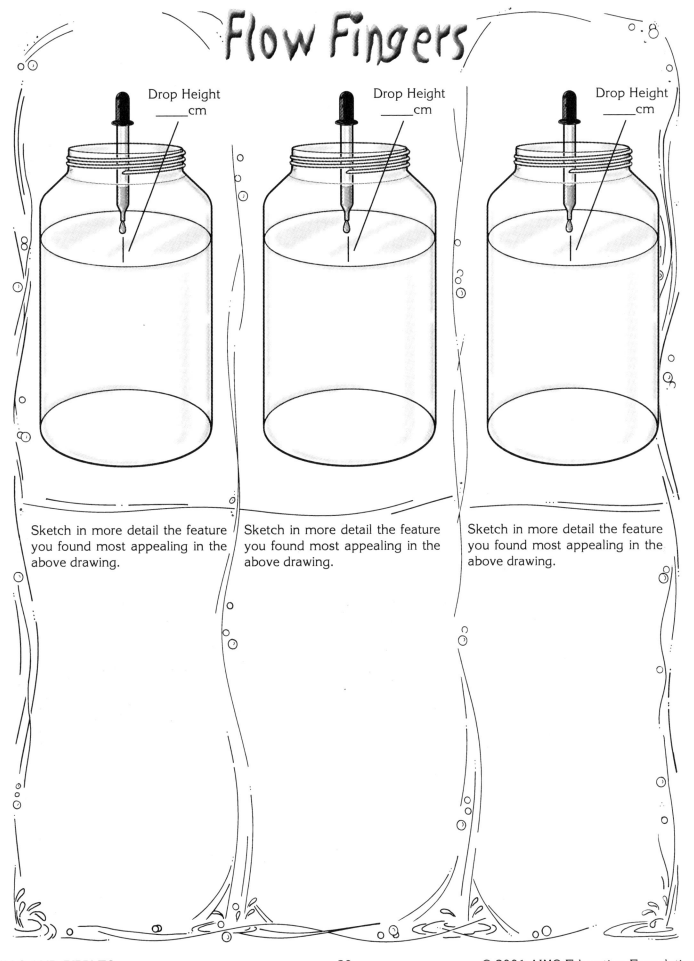

Drop Height _____ cm

Drop Height _____ cm

Drop Height _____ cm

Sketch in more detail the feature you found most appealing in the above drawing.

Sketch in more detail the feature you found most appealing in the above drawing.

Sketch in more detail the feature you found most appealing in the above drawing.

# Flow Fingers

| Time | Shape | Number of Tentacles | Distance from Top of Water Surface |
|---|---|---|---|
| | | | |
| | | | |
| | | | |
| | | | |
| | | | |
| | | | |
| | | | |

Time when color reaches bottom of container = _____ seconds

Time when water is uniformly colored = _____ minutes

| Time | Shape | Number of Tentacles | Distance from Top of Water Surface |
|---|---|---|---|
| | | | |
| | | | |
| | | | |
| | | | |
| | | | |
| | | | |
| | | | |

Time when color reaches bottom of container = _____ seconds

Time when water is uniformly colored = _____ minutes

# Fluid Instabilities and Complexity

The patterns produced by fluid instabilities in *Flow Fingers* provide an introduction to an exciting frontier of science—Complexity. The physics of Complexity involves describing which aspects of a complex phenomenon are predictable and which are not. Some of the description can be in words and then physicists try to quantify the description mathematically by developing equations that closely approximate the event. For example, some features of *Flow Fingers* are predictable, while others are not. The number of streamers that grow from the Widnall Instability of the vortex ring is usually between four and eight. That is predictable. But the exact number of streamers during each experiment is not predictable.

Another complex phenomenon is the weather. It has both predictable and random features. It's predictably cold in Los Alamos, NM during January, but the temperature on a given January day is unpredictable. The weather five minutes from now, wherever you are, is fairly predictable, but the weather in two weeks is far less predictable.

Another important aspect of Complexity and *Flow Fingers* is the variety of distances, also called "scales," that are relevant to describing the flow. In *Flow Fingers*, the vertical lengths of the streamers are several centimeters, and each "generation" of streamers and mushroom caps repeats every ten centimeters or so. The mushroom caps have dimensions of about one centimeter and the tentacles are a few millimeters thick. In order to describe this flow to someone who has never seen it, one must explain all of these "scales" and how they relate to each other. The more scales, the more complex is the event.

Because the *Flow Fingers* patterns are complicated, we might be tempted to call them "turbulent." An example of turbulence is the water motion near a motorboat's rapidly spinning propeller, where the water movement is dominated by *random motion*. *Flow Fingers* is not dominated by randomness although some of the flow is unpredictable. *Flow Fingers* patterns are not turbulent, but they are complex.

Fluid instabilities, including Rayleigh-Taylor Instability, often *lead* to turbulence even though the flow *during* the instability may not be turbulent. For example, in *Look Out Below!* RTI causes water to pour from an inverted jar. The water splashing into the tub or on the floor below can be turbulent until the water comes to rest. However, the flow is not turbulent during RTI when the small ripples at the water-over-air interface begin to grow into bigger ripples.

*Flow Fingers* demonstrates some important elements of Complexity: Some features are predictable while others are not. Phenomena occur on several different and distinct scales. Unpredictability and Complexity do not necessarily mean the flow is turbulent and random. Science research is now on the brink of understanding these concepts and their implications.

41

# LIQUID ROPE

## Topic
Flow patterns of mixing liquids

## Key Question
How can one liquid be "poured" into another liquid without mixing?

## Focus
Students will use an eyedropper to "pour" liquid food coloring into water and observe that the two liquids do not mix until the food coloring strikes the bottom of the container.

## Guiding Documents
*Project 2061 Benchmark*
- *The action of gravitational force on regions of different densities causes them to rise or fall—and such circulation, influenced by the rotation of the earth produces winds and ocean currents.*

*NRC Standard*
- *Develop descriptions, explanations, predictions, and models using evidence.*

*NCTM Standards 2000\**
- *Understand such attributes as length, area, weight, volume, and size of angle and select the appropriate type of unit for measuring each attribute*
- *Recognize and apply mathematics in contexts outside of mathematics*

## Math
Geometry and spatial sense
Measurement
    length
    time

## Science
Physical science
    fluid flow

## Integrated Processes
Observing
Predicting
Collecting and recording data

## Materials
*For each group:*
    clean, clear, plastic two-liter bottle with label removed
    glass eyedropper
    food coloring, several colors
    plastic spoon

## Background Information
To a physicist, the word *fluid* can be applied to either a liquid or a gas. Rayleigh-Taylor Instabilities (RTI) occur in fluids. In particular, they occur at the *interface* between fluids with different densities. The interface is where the different fluids meet.

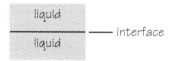

For example, cooking oil and water are both liquids. Cooking oil will float on water because its density is less than the density of water. The surface where the oil and water meet is called the *interface*.

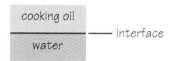

Cooking oil over water is an example of a *liquid/liquid* interface. Cooking oil over water is stable because the less dense fluid, the cooking oil, is over the more dense fluid, the water. RTI occurs when a higher-density fluid is on top of a lower-density fluid. In *Liquid Rope*, the higher-density fluid, food coloring, is on top of the lower-density fluid, the water. The higher-density fluid penetrating into the lower-density fluid is called a *Rayleigh-Taylor spike*.

In *Flow Fingers*, students observe RTI when the higer-density food coloring is on top of the lower-density water, just as we have in *Liquid Rope*, but the flow patterns are different because *Flow Fingers* uses a single drop of food coloring and *Liquid Rope* uses an eyedropper full of food coloring. When the drop of food coloring in *Flow Fingers* punches through the air/water interface, microscopic swirling occurs on the drop. This swirling (called vorticity) changes the way the Rayleigh-Taylor spikes form. The drop first becomes a wavy ring and then the spikes form. In *Liquid Rope*, there is no drop punching through an air/water interface, so no swirling occurs and the Rayleigh-Taylor spike forms immediately to start the thin column of food coloring falling through the water.

The Rayleigh-Taylor Instability is the effect that starts this flow. Once the stream of food coloring gets started, then the effect is simply a higher-density liquid (food coloring) falling through a lower-density liquid (water). So RTI occurs only at the very start of the food coloring leaving the dropper and becoming a stream falling through the water.

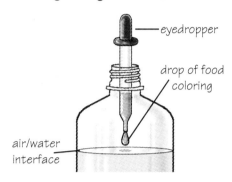

In *Liquid Rope*, the interface is liquid over liquid. The higher-density food coloring is over the lower-density water.

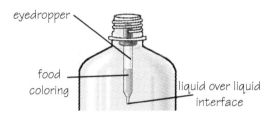

The narrow tip of the eyedropper slowly injects the food coloring into the water. The drop of food coloring in *Flow Fingers* strikes the air-over-water interface with a lot of energy. The food coloring in the tip of the eyedropper in *Liquid Rope* starts from rest. RTI occurs at the food coloring-water interface to start the flow. Assuming there are no currents in the water, the denser food coloring "falls" straight down. It's helpful to think of the food coloring as grains of sand and the streamline of food coloring as sand grains pouring from a container and falling straight to the ground. Mixing occurs when the streamline of food coloring strikes the bottom of the container.

## Management
1. Collect and save clean plastic spoons from fast food outlets.
2. Ask students to bring empty, clean, clear, two-liter bottles with the lables removed to class.
3. Divide the students into groups of three.
4. Provide paper towels to clean up spillage.

## Procedure
1. Assign one student from each group to fill a two-liter bottle so that the water level is up to the top of the bottle. Tell them to allow the water in the

bottle to sit undisturbed so that currents in the water have time to subside.
2. Distribute the *Liquid Rope Observations* page to each student.
3. Assign a different student in each group to squeeze 15 drops of food coloring into the bowl of the spoon. Tell them to squeeze the bulb on the eyedropper and pick up as much of the food coloring as the eyedropper will hold.
4. Instruct the students to slowly and carefully lower the eyedropper into the water and to release the eyedropper when the bulb is slightly above the water's surface. Tell them that the neck of the bottle will keep the eyedropper centered.

If the eyedropper bulb would fall through the bottle opening, then make a round hole in an index card just big enough for the eyedropper stem, put the eyedropper through the card, and place the eyedropper with card on the bottle, so the card keeps the eyedropper from falling in.
5. Have the students record the color and level of the food coloring in the eyedropper on their *Liquid Rope Observations* page.
6. Instruct the students to observe and record, over time, the behavior of the food coloring.
7. If time allows, let students repeat this process for different colors of food coloring.

## Discussion
1. A steady stream of food coloring is observed to flow from the tip of the eyedropper. What happens to the liquid level in the eyedropper?
2. What evidence is there that a mixing of water and food coloring is occurring in the barrel of the eyedropper?
3. Most packages of food coloring contain four different colors. Is there any difference in the behavior of different colors? Explain.
4. Rhythmically tap a finger on the surface on which the bottle is sitting. How does the food coloring flow change? [The thin streamline of food coloring will develop bead-like bulges. As these bulges fall, they will often separate from the streamline and form beautiful circular patterns. These patterns will often pass through each other.]

43

5. Compare the density of water with the density of the food coloring. [Food coloring, since it sinks in water, has a density greater than the density of water.]

**Extensions**
1. What effect does water temperature have on the food coloring streamline?
2. Can you create a liquid rope that is curved? Explain.

* Reprinted with permission from Principles and *Standards for School Mathematics*, 2000 by the National Council of Teachers of Mathematics. All rights reserved.

# LIQUID ROPE Observations

1. Record the color and level of the food coloring in the eyedropper by coloring the eyedropper in the first diagram.
2. Sketch the flow of the food coloring at the recorded time of observation.

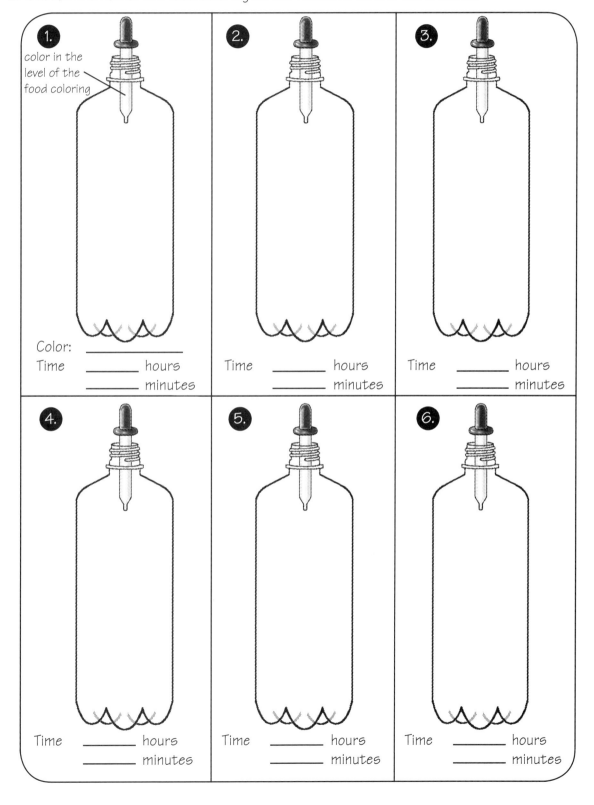

1.
color in the
level of the
food coloring

Color: _____
Time _____ hours
_____ minutes

2.
Time _____ hours
_____ minutes

3.
Time _____ hours
_____ minutes

4.
Time _____ hours
_____ minutes

5.
Time _____ hours
_____ minutes

6.
Time _____ hours
_____ minutes

# A Fluid-Dynamical Centerpiece
## An aesthetic application of Rayleigh-Taylor Instability

For that special dinner when a unique centerpiece is desired for the dinner table, consider Rayleigh-Taylor Instability. It produces inexpensive and innovative elegance as only fluid instabilities can. Start with a clear bottle, 12-15 inches tall. An unusually shaped bottle will provide a special touch, but a one- or two-liter clear bottle with a ribbon tied around the neck will do. About a half-hour before guests will be seated, fill the bottle with water and allow the water to rest. Place the bottle precisely where it will reside during dinner.

After the guests are seated, add a drop of food coloring to the water. It will drop through the water surface and momentarily become a ring of intense color before fingering into elegant plumes that cascade slowly downward, reminiscent of Fourth-of-July fireworks. The colors and patterns of fireworks right in your own home, bottled for all to see!

The cascade will continue for about 15 minutes before the color diffuses away. When the show is over, invite one of your guests to begin the next show with another drop of food coloring. The second drop may be the same color as the first or another hue. At least a half dozen shows can be watched before the water becomes too dark to see subsequent Rayleigh-Taylor cascades.

Colors may be selected randomly or coordinated with the dinner food or decor. Green cascades are a good match for salads and legumes, while red goes better with desserts, particularly berries and brightly colored ice cream or sorbet. Bon appetite!

# Soapy Spills

## Topic
The effect of surface tension on water/air interfaces

## Key Question
What happens to the water in a container with a gauze barrier when soap is added and the container is turned upside down?

## Focus
Students will systematically add liquid soap or detergent to the water in a container with a gauze barrier and explore the effect of lessening surface tension.

## Guiding Documents
*Project 2061 Benchmark*
- *The action of gravitational force on regions of different densities causes them to rise or fall—and such circulation, influenced by the rotation of the earth produces winds and ocean currents.*

*NRC Standards*
- *Objects have many observable properties, including size, weight, shape, color, temperature, and the ability to react with other substances. Those properties can be measured using tools, such as rulers, balances, and thermometers.*
- *Different kinds of questions suggest different kinds of scientific investigations. Some investigations involve observing and describing objects, organisms, or events; some involve collecting specimens; some involve experiments; some involve seeking more information; some involve discovery of new objects and phenomena; and some involve making models.*

*NCTM Standards 2000\**
- *Understand such attributes as length, area, weight, volume, and size of angle and select the appropriate type of unit for measuring each attribute*
- *Recognize and apply mathematics in contexts outside of mathematics*

## Math
Measurement
    volume
    area
    angle
Estimation
Statistics
    mean
    median
    range

## Science
Physical science
    matter
        fluids (liquids and gases)
            Rayleigh-Taylor Instability

## Integrated Processes
Observing
Collecting and recording data
Comparing and contrasting
Inferring

## Materials
*For each group:*
    plastic bucket for catching spilled water
    open-mouthed, rigid container (e.g., baby-food jar)
    rubber band
    five-inch square piece of cheesecloth or gauze
    eyedropper
    $\frac{1}{4}$ teaspoon measure
    liquid dish soap
    hand lens
    *Critical Angle Protractor*
    cardboard, 4" x 5"

## Background Information
Water does not spill from an inverted, gauze-covered jar because the gauze helps surface tension keep the water surface smooth. In the activity *Look Out Below!*, we observed that any of three barriers could "support" water in an upside-down jar, provided the barrier is supported during the process of turning the jar over. Water could be contained within a jar *sealed* with an index card, tissue paper, or gauze. In all three cases the air pressure equals the water pressure at the water/air interface, and the barrier aids surface tension to prevent ripples from forming. The absence of ripples stifles the Rayleigh-Taylor Instability which is responsible for water spilling from an inverted jar.

*Soapy Spills* investigates the role of surface tension in blocking Rayleigh-Taylor Instability (RTI). The gauze and surface tension keep ripples from forming at the interface between air and pure water, but the reduced surface tension in soapy water allows ripples to form. Easily formed ripples cause the surface of soapy water to be more fragile and more likely to spill water when shaken, even slightly. When ripples do form, they grow, producing drips or streams of water. A *robust* water surface resists spilling, but a *fragile* water surface spills easily when the jar is gently shaken or tilted. The amount of surface tension determines whether a water surface is robust or fragile because it influences the formation of ripples. The large surface tension of pure water keeps ripples from forming, but reduced surface tension of soapy water allows ripples to form easily.

Surface tension is caused by the bonding of molecules. Water molecules are made of two hydrogen atoms and one oxygen atom ($H_2O$). The hydrogen atoms of the water molecule are attracted to the oxygen atoms of other water molecules, forming a connection between them. This is called *hydrogen bonding*. Water molecules stick together like close friends.

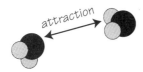

The water molecules under the water surface are pulled in all directions. But the molecules *at the* water surface, which is the air/water interface, are tugged only by molecules under the surface and by nearby molecules on the surface. The pull of air molecules on surface water molecules is very weak. The effect of water molecules on the surface being pulled strongly toward the bulk liquid is that the water surface behaves as if it has a film or skin. This effect is called *surface tension*. Surface tension keeps the surface of the water glassy smooth, making it difficult for ripples to form on the water surface. Without ripples, RTI does not occur, and so the water stays in the jar.

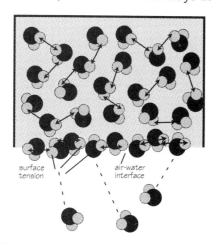

When liquid soap is added to the water, the soap molecules wedge themselves between the water molecules, weakening the hydrogen bonds. This effect decreases the surface tension at the air/water interface. With reduced surface tension, ripples form more easily, and they grow. This ripple growth is RTI, and it causes the water to spill from the jar.

In this activity, students will perform three different tests on the integrity of the water surface. They will specify an *Integrity Rating* using a 1–5 scale. A rating of 5 applies to the pure-water (no soap added) test. The 5-rating means the surface is rugged and

sturdy during the three tests. As soap is added, the surface becomes more and more delicate. A rating of 3 means that mild shaking causes the water to spill out, and a rating of 1 means the water runs out no matter how steady the jar is held.

## Management

1. Organize your students into groups of three or four.
2. Be sure to have containers available to catch water spills.
3. Have a good supply of paper towels or sponges on hand to absorb water spills.
4. Weather permitting, this activity can be done outdoors to minimize cleanup.
5. Measure the volume of one of the containers the students will be using. Subtract 50 mL from this volume. This will be the volume of water students will measure and pour into their containers.
6. Each group of students will need to construct one *Critical Angle Protractor.*

## Procedure

1. Assign one member in each group to organize the group's materials. Have this student wet the cheesecloth or gauze and then cover the open end of the container with it and secure it with a rubber band.

2. Assign a different student to measure the specified volume of water. Direct this student to add this volume to the container by carefully pouring it through the material covering the mouth of the jar.

3. Assign a third student to invert the container with cardboard or a plate to support the gauze, and then establish stability of the water/gauze/air interface. If any students spill an excessive amount of water, have them re-measure and again add the specified volume of water to their containers.

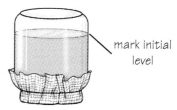

4. When the jar is inverted, have students perform the three tests and determine the integrity of the water surface on a 1–5 scale (see *Background Information*). Direct one student per group to hold the jar to do all three tests, while each of the other students in the group observes the tests and specifies on *Integrity Rating*. The three tests are: (1) blowing air across the water/gauze/air surface, (2) shaking the jar, (3) tilting the jar.

   After the student holding the jar has performed all three tests, instruct the other students in the group to determine the *Integrity Rating*. Then direct them to average the ratings within their group to get a single value for the data table. These integrity tests will be repeated each time more soap is added to the water.

5. Assign a student the task of adding a single drop of soap solution to the water. One way is to remove the gauze barrier, add the soap directly to the water, and stir the water gently to mix the soap. Warn the students not to stir so vigorously that many soap bubbles form on the surface. Another way to add soap is to pour out the water through the gauze into another container, add the soap to the water, stir the solution gently, and gently pour the soapy water back into the first container (pouring it through the gauze). If using this method, caution the students to pour the water back carefully enough to avoid creating soap bubbles on the gauze, because these bubbles may change the outcome.

   In any case, do not have students add soap by pouring the soap through the gauze because this creates a high concentration of soap at the water surface when the jar is inverted.

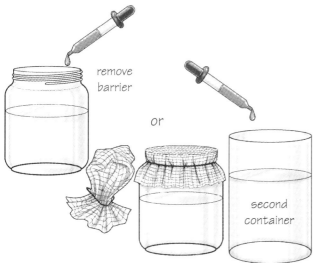

remove barrier

or

second container

6. After each addition of soap, have the students invert the jar, perform the tests, and determine the water surface integrity on the 1–5 scale. Also have them observe whether the water leaks by dripping out, by streaming, or by gushing from the jar.

Direct the students to record this observation in column, *Type of Leak*. Have them note when the water leaks out in a steady, continuous stream that cannot be stopped by steadying the jar. Direct them to catch the spilled, soapy water each time and re-use it by adding additional soap, as specified in step #5. If a few drops of soap have little effect, then add soap in units of $\frac{1}{4}$ teaspoon instead of drops.

7. Have students make a *Critical Angle Protractor* and measure the critical angle for each trial. The *critical angle* is the tilt angle when water begins to leak out, either as a steady stream of drops or as a stream.

8. When all data have been collected, have groups share their number of drops to get a steady stream. Direct them to determine the mean, median, and range for this data.

## Discussion

1. What did you notice about the "Surface Integrity" as more soap was added? Why do you think soapy water leaks out of the jar more easily than pure water?
2. Make a scatter graph with *Amount of soap added* on the horizontal axis and *Integrity Rating* on the vertical axis. What does this scatter graph tell you?
3. Why do you think we would want to know about the effects of soap on the surface of water?

## Extensions

1. Does the mesh size influence the amount of soap solution required to initiate leaking? The mesh can be made more coarse by cutting away some threads.
2. This experiment may be done with straws instead of a jar and gauze. Use straws of different diameters, such as straws used on water bottles for athletics. Dip the straw into a tall container of soapy water, put your finger on top, lift the straw with water inside, and observe that soapy water is more difficult to keep in the straw than pure water.

\* Reprinted with permission from *Principles and Standards for School Mathematics*, 2000 by the National Council of Teachers of Mathematics. All rights reserved.

# Critical Angle Protractor

**Construction:**
1. Copy or print this page on card stock or glue it to a piece of cardboard.
2. Cut out the Protractor piece and the Movable Arm.
3. Use a paper punch to put a hole in the Movable Arm.
4. Use a paper punch to make a pivot hole in each piece.
5. Attach the Movable Arm to the top of the Protractor with a paper fastener.

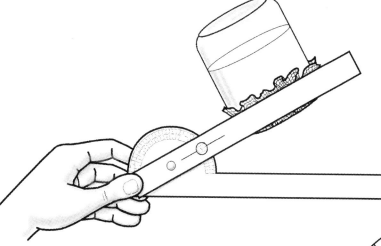

**Using the Critical Angle Protractor:**
1. Hold the Protractor in one hand as shown in the diagram. Rest the bottom arm on the edge of the plastic tub used to catch water spills.
2. As the student holding the inverted jar slowly turns the jar, adjust the Movable Arm so that its lower edge remains parallel to the mouth of the jar.
3. Read the angle on the Protractor scale through the hole on the Movable Arm.
4. The angle at which Rayleigh-Taylor Instability occurs is called the critical angle.

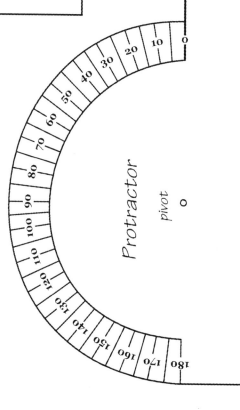

Spills Soapy

Lay your piece of barrier material over this millimeter grid and estimate the mesh size of the material.

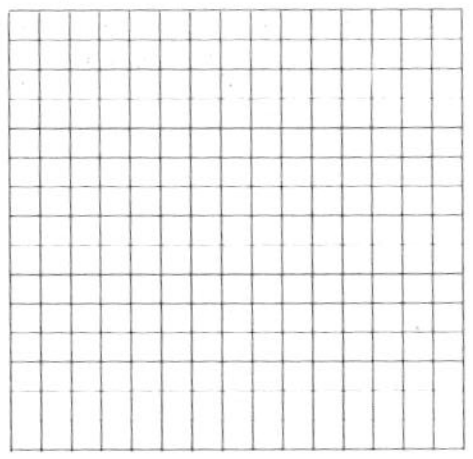

Mesh Size = _____ mm

_[millimeter grid]_

Tests:
a. Blow air across the water/gauze/air surface.
b. Gently shake the jar.
c. Tilt the jar.

Surface Integrity Scale

1 — 2 — 3 — 4 — 5
fragile         rugged

Type of leaks: **d**rips, **s**tream, **g**ush

## Group Data

| Number of Drops | Surface Integrity (scale of 1-5) | Critical Angle | Water Spilled (mL) | Type of Leak | Observations |
|---|---|---|---|---|---|
| 0 | 5 | | | | Pure water |
| | | | | | |
| | | | | | |
| | | | | | |
| | | | | | |

## Class Data

| Group | Number Of Drops to Get A Steady Stream |
|---|---|
| | |
| | |
| | |
| | |
| | |
| | |

Total _____

Class Mean _____ drops

Median _____ drops

Range _____ drops

Compare your group's number of drops to the class mean and median number of drops.

# BRACKISH WATER

## Topic
Mixing of fluids, Rayleigh-Taylor Instability

## Key Question
How do fresh water and salt water mix?

## Focus
Students will measure the mixing of fresh water and salt water for different amounts of salinity (saltiness) and will relate their results to the mixing of a river with ocean water.

## Guiding Documents
*Project 2061 Benchmark*
- *The action of gravitational force on regions of different densities causes them to rise or fall—and such circulation, influenced by the rotation of the earth produces winds and ocean currents.*

*NRC Standards*
- *Objects have many observable properties, including size, weight, shape, color, temperature, and the ability to react with other substances. Those properties can be measured using tools, such as rulers, balances, and thermometers.*
- *Different kinds of questions suggest different kinds of scientific investigations. Some investigations involve observing and describing objects, organisms, or events; some involve collecting specimens; some involve experiments; some involve seeking more information; some involve discovery of new objects and phenomena; and some involve making models.*

*NCTM Standards 2000\**
- *Understand such attributes as length, area, weight, volume, and size of angle and select the appropriate type of unit for measuring each attribute*
- *Recognize and apply mathematics in contexts outside of mathematics*

## Science
Physical science
    matter
        fluids, mixing
            Rayleigh-Taylor Instability

## Integrated Processes
Observing
Comparing and contrasting
Applying

## Materials
*For each group:*
    tray for containing any spilled water
    2 identical baby food jars, 6-oz.
    index cards, plastic-coated playing cards, or laminated cards
    2 single-serving salt packets
    water-base marker or food coloring, 2 colors
    plastic spoon
    sponge for cleanup of spilled water
    colored pencils
    transparent tape

## Glossary
- *Brackish*: salty, but not as salty as the seawater in the ocean
- *Fluid interface*: the boundary between two gases, two liquids, or a gas and a liquid
- *Rayleigh-Taylor Instability (RTI)*: the growth of ripples at the horizontal interface between two fluids when the higher-density fluid is on top
- *Salinity*: saltiness, briny
- *Turbulence*: fast fluid motion, usually associated with rapid mixing of fluids

## Background Information
Where the fresh water from a river mixes with the salt water of an ocean, the region is called "brackish water," implying that it's salty but not the full salinity of the ocean. Because salt water is more dense than fresh water, there's the possibility for fluid instability.

An interface between two liquids that are not flowing is either "stratified" or "unstable." If the higher-density liquid is on the bottom, the interface is stratified, meaning it doesn't change much. If the higher-density liquid is on the top, then the interface is unstable and Rayleigh-Taylor Instability can occur. This process is the growth of ripples at the interface, leading to mixing of the two liquids.

Where river water enters an ocean, these processes will occur if the river is not moving too rapidly. Rapid flow promotes turbulence and so the fresh water and salt water will mix by virtue of the turbulence rather than any fluid instability.

This activity looks at the mixing of fresh water and salt water when the water is not flowing. Students discover that when the fresh water is on top (i.e., higher-density liquid—salt water—is on bottom), the liquids are stratified so virtually no mixing occurs. However, when the salt water is on top, mixing occurs in less than one minute, even for fairly low salt concentration.

52

They will infer that a layer of fresh water may be formed over the salt water at the mouth of a river (if turbulence is not significant), but nature will not permit a saltwater layer above fresh water.

## Management

1. Collect single-serving salt packets from fast-food franchises. You have the option of asking students to label salt amounts in either grams or packet units.

2. Measure the mass of salt contained in 10 salt packets and divide by 10 to determine the average mass of the salt contained in one single-serving salt packet. Knowing the average mass of one salt packet makes it easy to construct a packet-to-grams and grams-to-packet conversion chart. The following chart was computed from a sample that yielded an average of 0.80 grams per packet. (Your sample may yield a slightly different average).

| packets | grams |
| --- | --- |
| 1 packet | 0.80g |
| 1/2 packet | 0.40g |
| 1/4 packet | 0.20g |
| 1/8 packet | 0.10g |

3. You have the option to have the students measure, compute, and construct their own group chart from a 10-packet sample.

4. For each group, place both jars on a tray. Have the sponge nearby for any spills.

5. Plastic or plastic-coated cards are preferred. Uncoated paper cards will swell soon after being wetted and will be difficult to insert and pull out from between the glass jars.

6. Removing the card from between the jars may seem difficult at first, but experience soon renders it easy because water adhesion (sticking) provides an effective sliding seal between brims and card. This seal minimizes leakage.

## Procedure

1. Tell students which option to use to record salt quantities, grams or packets.

2. Use the spoon (or edge of dry card) and a 3-inch square of paper and demonstrate to students how to divide a single packet of salt into fractions of a packet. Instruct students to practice on the contents from a single salt packet.

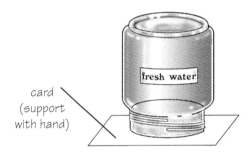

3. Tell students to fill one jar about one-half full with water. Have them add one-half packet of salt and mix until salt is dissolved. Direct

them to swish a water-base marker around in the water for a few seconds to color it or add one or two drops of food coloring. Instruct them to add water to fill the jar and then use the spoon to mix the water to a uniform color. Tell them to stick a piece of tape to the jar and label the jar as *salt water*.

4. Have the students fill the other jar with water and tint it with the second color. Instruct them to label the second jar *fresh water*.

5. Direct the students to cover the freshwater jar with the card and to carefully turn it upside down while holding the card firmly against the jar to contain the water.

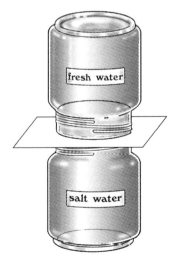

card
(support
with hand)

Instruct them to place this card and jar on the saltwater jar and align the jars so one is directly above the other. Tell students to wait 15 seconds and then caution them to slowly and carefully remove the card while keeping the jars aligned one above the other.

6. Ask students to observe whether the fresh water and salt water mix. Direct them to measure the

time that it takes to mix if mixing does occur and to record their observations.

7. Instruct students that to remove the upper jar without spilling, they should reinsert the card between the jars, lift the card and top jar as a unit, and turn it right-side-up. Tell students that if no mixing occurred, to add enough water to both jars until they're full, (if necessary) and put the card on the opening of the saltwater jar. If mixing occurred, have them discard the water in both jars and refill them according to steps 2 and 3.

8. Instruct students to carefully place the saltwater jar on top of the freshwater jar and, using the card to contain the saltwater, to slowly and carefully remove the card.

9. Tell students to observe whether the fresh water and salt water mix and, if mixing does occur, to measure the time that it takes to mix. Have them record their observations.

10. Instruct students that to remove the upper jar without spilling, they should reinsert the card between the jars and lift the top jar with card and turn it right-side-up. Tell students to discard the water in both jars.

11. Direct students to repeat the investigation using one packet of salt. Have them record their observations.

12. Have students repeat the investigation a fourth time using one-fourth packet of salt. Tell them to record their observations

## Discussion
1. What did you observe when you placed the fresh water on top of the salt water? [no mixing occurred]
2. How did that compare to the salt water on top of the fresh water? [mixing occurred]
3. Did the mixing time differ when you decreased the amount of salt? Explain.
4. Did the mixing time differ when you increased the amount of salt? Explain.

5. What effect did the method you used to remove the card have on the mixing rate? Explain.
6. What explanation do you have for why mixing occurs only when the salt water is on top? [The density of the salt water is greater than that of fresh water, so mixing occurs.]
7. How could you determine that salt water has a greater density than fresh water?
8. If a scuba diver is diving near the mouth of a river (where a river flows into an ocean), would he or she expect to start in fresh water near the surface and find salty water below? Explain.
9. Could the scuba diver start in salty water at the surface and encounter fresh water below? Explain.
10. If you're on a fishing boat in the ocean near the outflow of a large river and you run out of drinking water (fresh water), where would you look for more drinking water?

## Extensions
1. Ask interested students to make a stable freshwater over saltwater system and to then observe the system over a period of days (or even weeks) for any evidence of mixing.
2. Make a one-packet salt-water solution. Make a one-packet sugar-water solution (use fast-food sugar packets). How would you determine which solution was denser?
3. Challenge students to design an investigation to compare the densities of ice water and hot water.
4. Try using other fluids that you think are different in density. If you use sodas, make sure that the fizz (carbonation) is gone first.

*   Reprinted with permission from *Principles and Standards for School Mathematics*, 2000 by the National Council of Teachers of Mathematics. All rights reserved.

54

# BRACKISH WATER

1. **Fresh Water Over Salt Water**

   Describe what you observed when you placed the jar of fresh water on top of the jar of salt water. (Use colored pencils to illustrate the mixing you observed in each jar.)

| Top Jar | Bottom Jar | Amount of Salt (grams or packets) | Time to Mix |
|---------|-----------|-----------------------------------|-------------|
|         |           |                                   |             |

2. **Salt Water Over Fresh Water**

   Describe what you observed when you placed the jar of salt water on top of the jar of fresh water. (Use colored pencils to illustrate the mixing you observed in each jar.)

| Top Jar | Bottom Jar | Amount of Salt (grams or packets) | Time to Mix |
|---------|-----------|-----------------------------------|-------------|
|         |           |                                   |             |

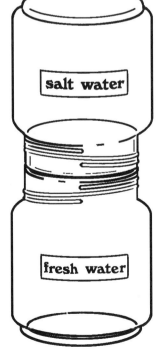

# BRACKISH WATER

### 3. Salt Water Over Fresh Water

Describe what you observed when you placed the jar of salt water on top of the jar of fresh water. (Use colored pencils to illustrate the mixing you observed in each jar.)

| Top Jar | Bottom Jar | Amount of Salt (grams or packets) | Time to Mix |
|---------|------------|-----------------------------------|-------------|
|         |            |                                   |             |

### 4. Salt Water Over Fresh Water

Describe what you observed when you placed the jar of salt water on top of the jar of fresh water. (Use colored pencils to illustrate the mixing you observed in each jar.)

| Top Jar | Bottom Jar | Amount of Salt (grams or packets) | Time to Mix |
|---------|------------|-----------------------------------|-------------|
|         |            |                                   |             |

# The Solar Pond
## An industrial application of blocking Rayleigh-Taylor Instability

Several activities in *Spills and Ripples* involve blocking Rayleigh-Taylor Instability so that water remains in an upside-down jar. Are there any industrial applications where blocking Rayleigh-Taylor Instability is beneficial? Yes! The operation of a Solar Pond depends on blocking Rayleigh-Taylor Instability.

The Solar Pond is a method to collect solar energy for use to generate electricity or heat large spaces. It converts sunlight into useful heat. A Solar Pond is clear so sunlight reaches the bottom, gets absorbed, and is converted to useful heat at the pond's floor. To understand the workings of a Solar Pond, we need to first understand how an ordinary pond warms and cools. It's helpful to think about a pond as having three layers of water: the top layer, middle layer, and bottom layer. There is no sharp separation between these layers, but the Solar Pond concept becomes more clear if we use this notion. Sunlight is absorbed at the pond's floor and heats the bottom layer of water.

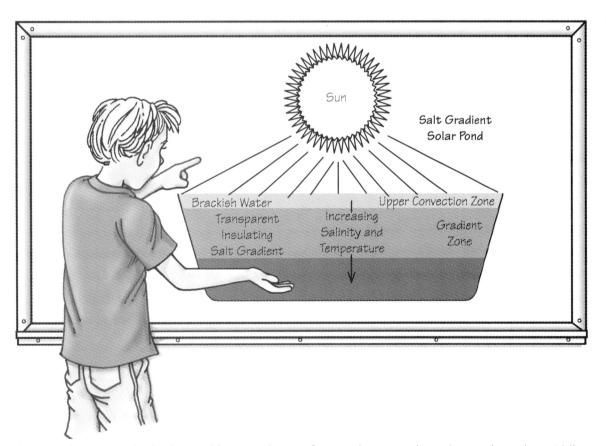

In an ordinary pond, the heated bottom layer of water becomes less dense than the middle layer. Because less-dense liquid (hot bottom layer) is below higher-density liquid (cooler middle layer), Rayleigh-Taylor Instability occurs and the warmer water mixes with the cooler water above. This process causes convection, the upward flow of heat via the upward motion of the warmed water. The heat that was absorbed in the bottom layer is rapidly distributed throughout the pond. When the heat reaches the top layer, it can be transported to the cooler air above or radiated away at night. The process of heating and cooling an ordinary pond depends on Rayleigh-Taylor Instability between the heated bottom layer and the middle layer.

A Solar Pond works by blocking Rayleigh-Taylor Instability at the interface between the middle and bottom layers. Without Rayleigh-Taylor Instability, the heat from sunlight goes into the bottom layer of water and the heat becomes trapped there. The bottom layer becomes very hot. The hot water of the bottom layer can then be pumped into machinery to heat large areas or to generate electricity. Another way to move the heat from the bottom layer to another place is to install pipes throughout the bottom layer and circulate a liquid through the pipes. The circulating liquid becomes heated by the hot bottom layer and is then pumped to a place where the heat is used industrially.

How does a Solar Pond block Rayleigh-Taylor Instability? The task is to keep the heated bottom layer of water from becoming less dense than the middle layer. This can be done by making the bottom layer very salty. Large amounts of salt are dissolved in the bottom layer, but not the middle or top layers. When the salty bottom layer is heated by sunlight, its density remains greater than the middle layer so Rayleigh-Taylor Instability does not occur at the interface between the middle and bottom layers, as it does in ordinary ponds. Thus, the middle and top layers remain cool while the bottom layer becomes very hot.

A Solar Pond requires maintenance. The water must be cleaned regularly so most of the sunlight irradiating the Solar Pond reaches the bottom layer. The water must be periodically changed because the salinity (saltiness) from the bottom layer slowly diffuses into the middle and top layers. When the middle layer becomes sufficiently saline, then the heated bottom layer can become less dense than the middle layer, so Rayleigh-Taylor Instability starts convection and the bottom layer cools by heating the rest of the pond, instead of trapping the heat. If pipes are used to remove the heat from the bottom layer, then leaks in the pipe must be repaired. Sending a diver down to fix the pipe isn't safe because the bottom layer is hot enough to cook the diver! The hot water must be removed or the Solar Pond must be cooled before a diver can safely make repairs. If Solar Ponds become plentiful in the future, perhaps robots that can work in hot water will be developed to do these repairs.

Discussions about Solar Ponds frequently neglect to mention Rayleigh-Taylor Instability because it's not yet a popular term. Engineers who work with Solar Ponds are concerned about the *convection* process that transports the heat rather than the Rayleigh-Taylor Instability that starts the convection process. So descriptions of Solar Ponds in books and on the web are not good places to learn about Rayleigh-Taylor Instability.

Solar Ponds can be built and used in areas where there is much sunlight, large tracts of undeveloped land, and an abundant supply of cheap salt. There are Solar Ponds in the Southwest U.S., India, and Israel.

# Mixing

One lesson from the results of "Brackish Waters" is that salt water above fresh water causes efficient mixing. At the mouth of a river, fresh water from the river is flowing into the salt water of the ocean. Would one expect to find a surface layer of salt water above the fresh water? No!—RTI mixing is too efficient! But would one expect to find a surface layer of fresh water above the salt water? Yes!—There is no RTI mixing because the lower-density liquid (fresh water) is on top, so the mixing must be caused by other effects, like swirling or diffusion. When people dive underwater at the mouth of a river, they sometimes notice that they sink easily for a few feet and then there is an unseen boundary where the water below the boundary is more buoyant than the water above. The boundary is the interface between the freshwater surface layer and the salt water below. For some large rivers flowing slowly into an ocean, the surface freshwater layer can extend for many miles over the salty ocean water.

There are other methods of mixing and some are more efficient than RTI while others are less so. For example, turbulent mixing is more efficient. It occurs when at least one of the fluids being mixed is moving rapidly and has lots of swirling. Using a spoon to stir cream into coffee is a common example of turbulent mixing, and it takes only a few seconds to produce a well-mixed solution of coffee and cream. One could also use RTI to mix cream into coffee by carefully pouring in the cream as a layer atop the coffee and watching it undulate as RTI produces mixing. Alternatively, one can carelessly add cream and wait for it to mix diffusively with the coffee. This will take quite a few minutes, more than most coffee drinkers prefer to wait. Diffusive mixing is less efficient than RTI.

# Oopsy Do

## Topic
Fluids, Rayleigh-Taylor Instability, Failure Analysis

## Key Question
When trying to contain water in an inverted bottle with a paper barrier, what is the connection between the type of paper used for the barrier and the manner in which the water spills from the bottle?

## Focus
Students will use a variety of ways to cause water to spill from a water-filled, inverted bottle with the opening covered by paper. They will carefully observe the failure mode. Students will correlate failure mode with causes of failure.

## Guiding Documents
*Project 2061 Benchmark*
- *The action of gravitational force on regions of different densities causes them to rise or fall—and such circulation, influenced by the rotation of the earth produces winds and ocean currents.*

*NRC Standards*
- *Objects have many observable properties, including size, weight, shape, color, temperature, and the ability to react with other substances. Those properties can be measured using tools, such as rulers, balances, and thermometers.*
- *Different kinds of questions suggest different kinds of scientific investigations. Some investigations involve observing and describing objects, organisms, or events; some involve collecting specimens; some involve experiments; some involve seeking more information; some involve discovery of new objects and phenomena; and some involve making models.*

*NCTM Standards 2000\**
- *Understand such attributes as length, area, weight, volume, and size of angle and select the appropriate type of unit for measuring each attribute*
- *Recognize and apply mathematics in contexts outside of mathematics*

## Science
Physical science
    matter
        fluids (liquids and gases)
            Rayleigh-Taylor Instability

## Integrated Processes
Observing
Comparing and contrasting
Collecting and recording data
Identifying and controlling variables
Analyzing

## Materials
One box each of several brands of facial tissue
One roll each of several brands of toilet paper
Empty bottles and jars of various shapes and sizes
Elastic bands
Index cards or laminated cards or any other flat surface large enough to cover the bottle openings

## Glossary (the meaning of words for this activity, not general usage)
- *Rayleigh-Taylor Instability (RTI):* the growth of ripples at an interface between two fluids when the upper fluid is more dense than the lower fluid, usually observed as pouring or spilling
- *Failure:* water escaping from an inverted bottle when we are trying to keep the water in the bottle
- *Failure Mode:* how the water exits the bottle, whether dripping, gushing, streaming, or glug-glug
- *Cause of Failure:* what happened that causes the water to leave the bottle (e.g., poking a hole or tearing the paper barrier)

## Background Information
Failures and unexpected results in science experiments and in engineering often lead to important learning and new insights. Accurate observation of how something fails is a crucial science-process skill and is the emphasis of this activity.

Students will try to contain water within an inverted bottle using a paper barrier (e.g., facial tissue or toilet paper) at the opening. The failure is water escaping from the bottle. Students will be asked to describe how the water flows when it spills or escapes (like dripping or streaming or gushing). How the water exits the bottle is the failure mode. The cause of failure is the type of hole or tear or rupture in the barrier that caused the water to spill out. When a water-filled, open bottle is turned upside down, the interface between the water in the bottle and the air below is fragile. The water and air pressures are equal at the water-over-air interface. However, Rayleigh-Taylor Instability (RTI) usually enables the water to escape. RTI is the growth of ripples at the water-over-air interface. Small ripples quickly grow into a stream or gush of downward-moving water. We usually describe this simply as water spilling from the bottle.

If the bottle opening is small (less than about 9 mm inside diameter), the water will stay in the bottle if the inversion process is done carefully and the bottle is not shaken or tilted. Surface tension keeps ripples from forming and so RTI is blocked. The water-over-air interface is in unstable equilibrium. For larger openings, surface tension is usually inadequate to smooth the ripples and so the ripples grow rapidly into a stream of falling water. We usually cannot observe the growth of ripples because it happens so quickly. Instead we simply observe that the water spills out.

The water-over-air interface can be made more sturdy by covering the bottle opening with facial tissue. The combination of wet tissue and surface tension causes smoothing of the water-tissue-air interface that suppresses ripple formation, so water can be contained within a bottle with a fairly large opening (over 10 cm diameter if done skillfully). However, the tissue may fail by itself, causing the water to spill, or it may be forced to fail. For example, a rupture in the tissue or sudden change in water pressure will likely create failure and spills.

When failure occurs, the water may spill from the bottle in several different ways, known as *failure modes*. It may drip out or form a steady stream. It may exit in a glug-glug-glug way. It may catastrophically come out in a large gush. The students' goal is to observe these different failure modes and determine what causes them. Is the failure mode a predictable consequence of the type of barrier, something about the bottle, or the cause of failure? Students will try a variety of papers to do this failure-mode analysis.

This activity is related to paper engineering. Paper engineers are concerned about the wet-strong property of paper, meaning how elastic and strong the paper is when wet. For bottle openings greater than about 5 cm inside diameter, the students will observe a difference between the wet-strengths of facial tissue and toilet paper. Toilet paper usually fails more easily than facial tissue. Facial tissue is engineered to be elastic and strong when wet whereas toilet paper is engineered to come apart when wet. The wet toilet paper will spontaneously tear over bottles with wide openings because it lacks the elasticity and strength of facial tissue. Also, generic-brand facial tissue will usually fail more easily than name-brand tissue. Sometimes inexpensive facial tissue is less elastic than name-brand toilet paper. Students should note these differences.

## Management

1. This activity is best done outdoors to avoid cleanup of spills. If it is done indoors, do each test over a sink or tub to catch spills.

2. Each test should be done with single-ply paper (tissue, toilet paper). If the paper is two-ply, instruct students to separate the layers and use only one layer for the test.

3. Look for empty bottles that once contained mouthwash, soda, jam, fruit juice, etc., as well as wide-mouth canning jars.

4. Help the students understand that careful failure-mode analysis constitutes success. Success and failure are not opposites in this context. The barrier fails to contain the water. The student succeeds by accurately observing and recording the barrier's failure.

5. This activity is best done by small groups of students, two to four per group.

6. Each group should use the same bottle and vary paper for about five tests before testing another bottle type with various papers.

## Procedure

1. Instruct students to select a bottle and a paper. Tell them to begin with a name-brand facial tissue and to only use a single-ply of the facial tissue. If it comes in two-ply or three-ply (as most do), then separate the layers and use only one layer for the test.

2. Instruct students to fill the bottle with water and cover the opening with the facial tissue. Tell them to allow the facial tissue to soak and then to carefully smooth the tissue over the opening. Inform them that if it tears, to remove it and install a new tissue. Suggest to students that a rubber band may be used to secure the tissue to the bottle's neck, but it's not necessary.

3. Direct students to use the palm of their hand or another flat surface (e.g., an index card), to support the bottle opening while gently turning the bottle upside down. Caution them that, if indoors, they need to hold the inverted bottle over a sink or tub to catch spills.

4. Tell students to wait about five seconds or longer for the water sloshing to stop, then to carefully remove their hand or flat surface so that the wet paper is the only barrier keeping the water in the bottle. Have them observe whether the water stays in. Tell them that if the water spills out, to observe the failure mode, the cause of failure, and the time it takes for the bottle to empty. Have them record these observations on the student sheet.

5. Instruct students that if the water stays in the bottle for at least 15 seconds, they should try causing the water to spill in a careful, controlled, observable way. For example, tell them to try poking a pencil through the tissue or to tear it by slitting it or creating a tear near the rim.

6. Ask students to carefully observe how the tissue fails and how the water escapes from the bottle. Have them record these observations.

7. Instruct students to do additional tests with other bottles or other papers. Suggest that each group should use each bottle for at least five tests with different papers.

## Discussion

1. What differences were found between the failures of the facial tissue and toilet paper, particularly for wide openings (greater than 5 cm inside diameter)? Noting that tissue is designed to confine sneezes and toilet paper is designed to disintegrate when wet, how can you explain these differences?
2. Did the failure mode depend on the opening size or shape of the bottle? Explain.
3. What are the limitations in using paper to contain water in an even larger-opening bottle (say, 8-inch diameter opening)?

## Extensions

1. Try different brands of paper towels and other papers.
2. Use a 20X microscope to examine samples of the facial tissue and toilet paper that you used for tests. Can you see differences in their fabric? Does the microscopic examination help you understand why they behave differently in Rayleigh-Taylor tests?
3. Try different shaped bottles to see whether the bottle shape influences the failure modes.

* Reprinted with permission from *Principles and Standards for School Mathematics*, 2000 by the National Council of Teachers of Mathematics. All rights reserved.

# Oopsy Do

# Menu

| Type of Paper | What Action Causes the Failure<br>Cause of Failure | What Does the Failure Look Like?<br>(how water leaves the bottle)<br>Failure Mode |
|---|---|---|
| facial tissue<br>toilet paper<br>paper towel<br>_____<br>_____ | poked small hole in paper<br>poked large hole in paper<br>cut a slit in paper<br>squeezed bottle<br>spontaneous<br>big slosh while inverting bottle<br>tore paper near rim of bottle<br>_____<br>_____ | drip<br>stream<br>glug-glug<br>gush<br>stop and start<br>_____<br>_____ |

|  | Test 1 | Test 2 | Test 3 |
|---|---|---|---|
| Description of Bottle or Jar |  |  |  |
| Diameter of Opening (cm) |  |  |  |
| Type of Paper Used as Barrier |  |  |  |
| Paper Brand |  |  |  |
| Failure Mode |  |  |  |
| Cause of Failure |  |  |  |

# Wet Papers

Papers are carefully engineered for different applications. We usually think of engineering in relation to machinery, but the engineering of paper is among the most important engineering achievements we encounter every day. Just think of how many different ways you use paper during a single day!

The purposes of various absorbent papers are different, and these differences become clearer when we use the paper to block Rayleigh-Taylor Instability. **Tissue** is designed to wipe spills and also to confine wet sneezes. It is engineered to have a high "wet-strength." The tissue fibers stay strong, even when wet. Experience shows that the name brands generally have a better wet strength than generic brands. Name-brand tissues can block Rayleigh-Taylor Instability over a jar opening of 10-cm diameter and greater because it is so good at keeping ripples from forming. Generic-brand tissues usually fail to confine water in a jar with a 10-cm opening.

However, **toilet paper** is designed to disintegrate when wet so it won't clog drain pipes or septic systems. Therefore, toilet paper is less effective at blocking Rayleigh-Taylor Instability. When it covers an upside-down jar of water and it tears, as it does easily when it's wet, it causes ripples to form so Rayleigh-Taylor Instability occurs and the water spills easily, usually in a huge gush.

**Paper towels** and **napkins** are different than tissues and toilet paper when wet. Some paper towels are designed with high wet-strength whereas others are designed to be extremely absorbent by swelling as it absorbs water. Likewise, some napkins have fairly good wet-strength while others tear easily.

The classic "Rayleigh-Taylor Instability test" of using paper to confine water in an upside-down jar is a good way to measure the relative wet-strengths of papers. Perhaps you can design other tests.

# DENSITY Dealings

## Topic
Relative density of solids and liquids

## Key Question
How will solids and liquids of different densities arrange themselves when combined?

## Focus
Students will measure the mass and volume of three liquids to determine relative densities. The placement of several solids in these liquids will help to determine the approximate densities of these solids.

## Guiding Documents
*Project 2061 Benchmarks*
- *When people care about what is being measured or counted, it is important to say what the units are.*
- *Make sketches to aid in explaining procedures or ideas.*
- *Equal volumes of different substances usually have different weights.*

*NRC Standards*
- *Employ simple equipment and tools to gather data and extend the senses.*
- *Use mathematics in all aspects of scientific inquiry.*

*NCTM Standards 2000\**
- *Represent, analyze, and generalize a varity of patterns with tables, graphs, words, and, when possible, symbolic rules*
- *Understand such attributes as length, area, weight, volume, and size of angle and select the appropriate type of unit for measuring each attribute*
- *Recognize and apply mathematics in contexts outside of mathematics*

## Math
Rational numbers
   decimals
Measurement
   mass
   volume

## Science
Physical science
   relative density

## Integrated Processes
Observing
Predicting
Collecting and recording data
Comparing and contrasting
Interpreting data

## Materials
*Part One*
   student sheet for *Part One*
   small cups, three per group
   masking tape or labels
   balances
   corn oil
   corn syrup
   water
   3 oral syringes marked in milliliters
   calculators

*Part Two*
   student sheet for *Part Two*
   graduated cylinders (or other narrow-diameter containers), one per group
   four to five small items made of different materials per group, such as:
      pieces of pink eraser
      pieces of gum or art erasers
      paper clips
      plastic chips
      toothpicks
      birthday candles

## Background Information
Density is a measure of the "compactness" of a material. The ratio of mass to volume for any material measured in grams per cubic centimeter ($g/cm^3$), density tells how much matter is packed into a given space. Density is not a simple comparison of the "heaviness" or "lightness" of materials. It is a comparison of the "heaviness" or "lightness" of the same amounts (mass per unit volume) of materials. The mistake most people make in thinking about density is to consider only size or mass instead of both of them together. When dealing with density, mass *and* volume always go hand in hand.

The density of materials is determined by the masses of the atoms in the material *and* the amount of space between the atoms. Gases have low densities not only because the atoms making up the gases have a small mass, but also because there is a large amount of space between the atoms. The heavy metals like gold, lead, and uranium are very dense because their atoms are massive *and* spaced closely together.

Water has a density of one gram per cubic centimeter at four degrees Celsius and is the standard for comparing the density of materials. Any solid or liquid material with a density greater than one $g/cm^3$ is more dense than water and will sink in water. Likewise, a solid or liquid material with a density less than one $g/cm^3$ will float in water.

## Management

*Part One*
1. Have students work in groups of three to six.
2. Each group needs three small cups for their liquids. Label these cups ahead of time with masking tape or small, peel-off labels.
3. Students will need to use balances to determine the masses of the cups both before and after they have added the liquids. Accuracy of these measurements is very important, so be sure that students know and understand how to use the balances to accurately determine mass.
4. Because this activity uses several messy liquids, set up three separate dispensing stations in areas of the classroom that can easily be cleaned after the activity is over. Each station should have the liquid in an open container that can be easily accessed with the oral syringe placed at that station.
5. Oral syringes are great tools for accurately measuring small amounts of liquid. They can be found in drug stores, veterinary clinics, and farm supply stores. The syringes for this activity need to have measurements marked out in milliliters. If you do not have access to oral syringes, graduated cylinders may be used instead, but this is a less accurate and messier alternative. If you do use graduated cylinders, be sure to have a ladle or spoon of some sort at the stations with corn syrup and corn oil to use when putting those liquids into the cylinders.
6. Before beginning the activity, develop a plan for rotating students through the dispensing stations so that each group ends up with containers of all three liquids.
7. The amounts of liquid that each group places in their cups are not important as long as they are consistent for all three liquids. Any amount between 30 and 50 milliliters will work well. Stress the importance of accuracy in these measurements.
8. Students can use calculators when computing the densities of the three liquids. Round densities to the nearest tenth.

*Part Two*
1. Each group will need one clear container that is at least 15 cm tall. Graduated cylinders or other similar

narrow-diameter containers (such as olive jars) work well and reduce the amount of each liquid required.
2. Develop a clean-up plan before starting this part of the activity—the oil and corn syrup should not be poured down the sink when students are through.
3. Each group will need four or five small items of differing densities to drop in their container. A few suggestions have been given in the *Materials* section, but don't feel limited to those ideas. Be sure to have at least one item that will stay above the oil, one that will stay between the oil and the water, one that will stay between the water and the syrup, and one that will sink all the way to the bottom. Each group should have the same items.
4. The items all need to be small enough to fit easily into the container that students are using and pass by each other no matter what order they are dropped in. Remind students to wait for one item to come to rest before dropping the next one in.

## Procedure

*Part One*
1. Divide the class into groups and explain the process for finding the densities of the three liquids.
2. Hand out the student sheet for *Part One* and three cups to each group.
3. Have students identify each of their cups with the appropriate label: water, corn syrup, and corn oil.
4. Direct students to find and to record the mass of each of their group's containers.
5. Rotate groups through the dispensing stations, having them take turns filling their containers. Remind students that they need to use the same volume for each liquid and maintain as much accuracy in their measurements as possible.
6. When groups have filled all three containers, urge them to carefully find the mass of each liquid and its container and record this information. To find the mass of the liquid, the mass of the container alone should be subtracted from the mass of the container and liquid together.
7. Have them use the mass and volume measurements to calculate the density of each liquid and fill in this information on the student sheet.
8. When students have completed the table, be sure that they answer the questions and draw a diagram of their prediction for what will happen when all three liquids are placed in the same container.
9. Invite students to share their results with the class to see how close the density calculations are from group to group. Discuss this process. If there are any great discrepancies, try to determine the reasons for these discrepancies.

*Part Two*
1. Hand out the student sheet for *Part Two* and a graduated cylinder or container to each group.

2. Have groups pour the liquids from their cups into the larger container in order from greatest to least density (first corn syrup, then water, then corn oil), and draw a diagram of these liquids in the container.

3. Give each group four or five items to drop into their container. Be sure that students make their predictions before dropping the items in.

4. Have groups drop their items into their containers one at a time, reminding them to let the previous object come to a complete stop before dropping in the next one. Gently tap or shake the container to keep the item falling through the liquids from sticking to the wall.

5. When all of the items are in the containers, have groups draw diagrams of the containers and the location of the items within them.

6. Close with a time of class discussion in which students compare their predictions and share what they have learned about density from this activity.

## Discussion

*Part One*

1. Which liquid has the greatest density? [corn syrup] ...the least? [corn oil] How do you know? [Look at the masses of the same volumes of liquids. Greatest mass for that volume will have the greatest density.]

2. Is that what you would have predicted before doing this activity? Why or why not?

3. How do the values for the densities of the liquids compare from group to group?

4. What are some possible reasons that account for these differences? Which values do you think are the most accurate?

5. What do you think would happen if all three liquids were placed in the same container? Why?

*Part Two*

1. How did the liquids look when they were all in the same container? [Corn syrup was on the bottom, water in the middle, and corn oil on the top.]

2. Was this the same or different from what you predicted in *Part One*? Explain.

3. Where did each item you dropped in come to rest in the container?

4. Would it make a difference if you had dropped the items in a different order? [No.] Explain. [As long as they are free to pass each other, they will always go to the same place because of their densities.]

5. How close were your predictions to the actual locations of the items?

6. What information would have helped you be more accurate in your predictions? [knowing the density of each item]

7. What does the location of each item tell you about its density? [It is more dense than any liquid it sinks through, but less dense than any liquid it stays above.]

8. What would happen if everything were mixed up and allowed to settle? [Eventually most liquids that are not miscible in each other and solids would go back to the way they originally were. If water and corn syrup are stirred together vigorously, they mix together and become one liquid, so there would no longer be a boundray between the water and corn syrup, even if we wait a long, long time. But the corn oil can never be mixed with water or corn syrup, so it will always "settle out" as a separate layer.]

9. What have you learned about density from this activity?

## Extensions

1. Select other liquids and find their relative densities.

2. Use other solid objects to place in the container.

3. Calculate the densities of the solid objects placed in the containers by finding their volumes (using a graduated cylinder and water displacement) and masses.

* Reprinted with permission from *Principles and Standards for School Mathematics*, 2000 by the National Council of Teachers of Mathematics. All rights reserved.

## Part One

### Instructions

a. Label your three cups: water, corn oil, and corn syrup.

b. Find the mass of each cup and record it in the table.

c. Go to each dispensing station and fill the appropriate cup with a small amount of each liquid. Be as accurate and consistent as possible. Record the volume in milliliters in the table. This value **must** be the same for all three liquids.

d. Find the mass of each cup with the liquid and record the total mass.

e. Determine the mass of each liquid without the cup, and using that value calculate the density of the water, corn oil and corn syrup. Remember that the density of a material is equal to its mass divided by its volume.

| | Mass of Empty Cup (Grams) | Volume of Liquid (Milliliters) | Mass of Cup with Liquid (Grams) | Mass of Liquid only (Grams) | Density of Liquid (Mass ÷ Volume) (Grams/Milliliter) |
|---|---|---|---|---|---|
| Water | | | | | |
| Corn oil | | | | | |
| Corn Syrup | | | | | |

1. Which liquid has the greatest density? ...the least density?

2. Does this surprise you? Why or why not?

3. What would happen if you put all three of the liquids into the same container? Draw and label a diagram of how you think it would look.

## Part Two

**Instructions**

a. Pour the three liquids from your cups in *Part One* into your group's large container in the following order: the liquid with the greatest density first, followed by the next greatest, with the least dense liquid last.

b. Draw and label your container.

1. How does this picture compare to the one you drew in *Part One*?

2. Predict what will happen to each of the items your teacher has for your group when you drop them into the container.

| Item | Prediction |
| --- | --- |
| a. _____ | _____ |
| b. _____ | _____ |
| c. _____ | _____ |
| d. _____ | _____ |
| e. _____ | _____ |

3. Drop the items into the container one at a time. Wait for each item to stop moving before dropping in the next one.

4. Draw and label a diagram of your container with its contents. How does the actual position of each item compare to your predictions?

# HIPPO HYDROMETER

## Topic
Specific gravity

## Key Question
How can we build and use a hydrometer to measure the relative density of various liquids?

## Focus
Students will make a simple hydrometer, calibrate it to water, and then compare its floating height in various liquids.

## Guiding Documents
*Project 2061 Benchmark*
- *The action of gravitational force on regions of different densities causes them to rise or fall—and such circulation, influenced by the rotation of the earth produces winds and ocean currents.*

*NRC Standards*
- *Objects have many observable properties, including size, weight, shape, color, temperature, and the ability to react with other substances. Those properties can be measured using tools, such as rulers, balances, and thermometers.*
- *Different kinds of questions suggest different kinds of scientific investigations. Some investigations involve observing and describing objects, organisms, or events; some involve collecting specimens; some involve experiments; some involve seeking more information; some involve discovery of new objects and phenomena; and some involve making models.*

*NCTM Standards 2000\**
- *Represent, analyze, and generalize a variety of patterns with tables, graphs, words, and, when possible, symbolic rules*
- *Select and apply techniques and tools. Accurately find length, area, volume, and angle measures to appropriate levels of precision*
- *Recognize and apply mathematics in contexts outside of mathematics*

## Science
Physical science
   density
      specific gravity

## Integrated Processes
Observing
Predicting

Comparing and contrasting
Hypothesizing

## Materials
*For each group:*
   tray for containing any spilled liquids
   1 clear plastic drinking straw
   3 clear plastic 10-ounce cups
   small, marble-size ball of plastic clay
   3 BBs
   granulated sugar
   cooking oil
   salt
   whole milk
   2% milk
   corn syrup
   paper towels

## Glossary
- *Density:* the ratio of mass to volume. The density of water is 1 gram per cubic centimeter. The mass of one cubic centimeter ($cm^3$) of water is one gram. Cooking oils have a density about 0.9 grams per $cm^3$.
- *Specific gravity:* the ratio of a material's density to the density of water. Specific gravity has no units. The specific gravity of water is 1.0. The specific gravity of cooking oils is about 0.9.
- *Hydrometer:* an instrument for measuring specific gravity of liquids.
- *Fluid:* a liquid or gas.
- *Rayleigh-Taylor Instability (RTI):* the growth of ripples at an interface between two fluids when the upper fluid is more dense than the lower fluid. It is usually observed as pouring or spilling.

## Background Information
Hydrometers of various kinds were used by the ancient Greeks, but the modern hydrometer was invented about 300 years ago. The English scientist, Robert Boyle (1627-1691), invented the glass hydrometer consisting of a long-stemmed glass bubble. He made many other contributions to the study of liquids and gases.

The hydrometer is a type of instrument that is made, then calibrated, then adjusted and re-calibrated. It is calibrated using common liquids of known specific gravity, and then it can be used to investigate a "mystery liquid" by measuring its specific gravity. The hydrometer calibration should be checked before and after each measurement of a mystery liquid. This procedure is good practice for science process skills.

A hydrometer works on the principle of flotation. The hydrometer is built to float in various liquids to be tested. When the hydrometer is placed in a liquid, part of it is above the liquid's surface and part is below. The hydrometer part below the liquid surface is called the "submerged" part. The hydrometer "reading" is the number on the hydrometer's scale closest to the liquid surface.

How does a hydrometer work? If a container is filled to the top by a liquid and then the hydrometer is placed in the liquid, some of the liquid will spill out in order to make room for the submerged part of the hydrometer. The spilled liquid is called the "displaced liquid." The volume of the displaced liquid is the same as the volume of the submerged part of the hydrometer. The principle of flotation is that the weight of the displaced liquid is equal to the weight of the entire hydrometer. When the hydrometer is placed in liquids of different densities, it displaces the same weight of each liquid because the weight of the hydrometer is always the same. Because the liquids have different densities, the volume of displaced liquid will be different for each liquid. So the volume of the submerged part of the hydrometer will be different for liquids of different densities. Consequently the hydrometer readings will be different, and it's this effect that makes it a useful instrument.

Let's look at the difference between the hydrometer floating in corn oil and corn syrup. When the hydrometer floats in corn oil (density 0.9 g/cm³), it displaces a certain amount of corn oil. The weight of displaced corn oil equals the weight of the hydrometer. When it floats in corn syrup that has a higher density, 1.3 g/cm³, it displaces less volume of corn syrup than corn oil. It displaces the same weight of corn syrup, but this weight of corn syrup occupies less volume than the same weight of corn oil. This happens because corn syrup has a higher density than corn oil. Because less volume of corn syrup is displaced, less of the hydrometer is submerged, so it rides higher in corn syrup than corn oil. The reading scale has low numbers on the bottom and high numbers on top, so the reading for corn syrup is lower than for corn oil.

## Management

1. BBs can be purchased at most sporting goods stores or in the sporting goods department of large retail stores. Make students accountable for the BBs issued to their group.
2. Inexpensive plastic trays for spill control like those used in fast-food restaurants can be purchased at any large retail store. Alternatively, students can make trays from shoebox tops by lining them with aluminum foil or plastic wrap to contain any spilled liquid.
3. To save on consumable materials, place cups of cooking oil, corn oil, whole milk, and 2% milk at one or more stations located around the classroom.

4. Decide whether to make the salt and sugar water solutions before teaching the lesson or to have the students prepare the solutions. Add four teaspoons of salt to each 10-ounce cup of water to make a saltwater solution. Add four teaspoons of sugar to each 10-ounce cup of water to make a sugar-water solution.
5. Copy the *Hippo Hydrometer Scales* page and cut out one scale for each group of students.
6. Use a plastic-based clay. Ordinary modeling clay will dissolve in water. Roll one marble-sized clay ball for each group.
7. Review the concepts of density and specific gravity with students.
8. Organize students into groups of three or four.

## Procedure

*Making and Calibrating the Hippo Hydrometer*

1. Distribute one *Making A Hydrometer* page to each group of students. Demonstrate to the students how to make a hydrometer.
2. Distribute one plastic straw, three BBs, one plastic cup, one clay ball, one hydrometer scale, and several sheets of paper towel to each group. Instruct the students to carefully follow the instructions through step six.
3. Show the students how to calibrate the hydrometer in a cup of water. Demonstrate how to dry the hydrometer with a paper towel.
4. Instruct one person in each group to fill the plastic cup with water. Have each student practice calibrating the hydrometer as described in steps seven and eight on the page.

*Using the Hippo Hydrometer*

1. Distribute one *Hippo Hydrometer Record* page and one *Hippo Hydrometer Graph* page to each student.
2. Distribute the liquids to each group or place in stations.
3. Have the students locate the labeled point on the graph (15, 1) that represents the specific gravity of water.
4. Inform students that the specific gravity of corn syrup is close to 1.3. Have them place the hydrometer in corn syrup and record the scale reading in the chart. (A calibrated hydrometer should float at a level close to 6 scale units.) Have students locate and label this point on the graph.
5. Inform the students that the specific gravity of cooking oil is close to 0.9. Have them place the hydrometer in cooking oil and record the scale reading in the chart. (A calibrated hydrometer should float at a level close to 18 scale units.) Have students locate and label this point on the graph.
6. Instruct the students to draw the straight line through the three points on the graph.

7. Tell the students to place the hydrometer in salt water and record the hydrometer scale units. Instruct them to locate that scale reading on the horizontal axis of the graph, go straight up to the line, move horizontally to the left, and read the specific gravity on the vertical axis. Show students how to position the corner of a sheet of paper on the graph of the line to make it easier to read either scale.

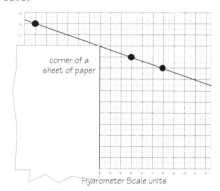

corner of a sheet of paper

Hydrometer Scale units

Have students record the specific gravity of salt water.

8. Instruct the students to repeat step seven for the other liquids. Caution them to check the calibration of the hydrometer by checking that the scale reading is 15 scale units when the hydrometer is is placed in the water. The water reading should be checked BEFORE and AFTER each reading in another liquid. Thus the correct procedure for each reading in other liquids is:
   • Place the hydrometer in water and adjust the scale to 15 if needed.
   • Wipe the hydrometer dry.
   • Place the hydrometer in the other liquid and read the scale number at the liquid level.
   • Wipe the hydrometer dry.
   • Place the hydrometer in water.
   • If the reading is still 15 scale units without adjusting the scale, then the reading in the other liquid is okay. If the reading in water is not 15, then adjust the scale to make it 15 and repeat the reading in the other liquid after wiping the hydrometer dry. "Calibration" here means to check that the hydrometer in water reads 15 scale units both before and after a measurement in another liquid.

## Discussion

1. Explain the meaning of *specific gravity.*
2. Why does specific gravity have no units? [Because it's defined to be the ratio of like quantities (densities). For example, the ratio of $10 to $1 is 10 to 1 or simply 10.] (Because specific gravities are relative densities and therefore unitless, the assignment of scale values is purely arbitrary. Traditionally, specific gravities less than 1.0 were

assigned negative values. This activity assigns the scale value of 15 to the specific gravity of water to keep from having negative numbers on the scale.)
3. Have the students compare their graph to this graph.

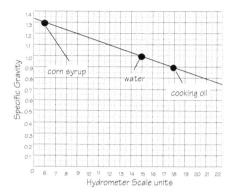

4. Have students compare their record chart to this one.

| Liquid | Hydrometer Units | Specific Gravity |
|---|---|---|
| Water | 15 | 1.0 |
| Corn Syrup | 6 | 1.3 |
| Cooking Oil | 18 | 0.9 |
| Saltwater Solution | 12 | 1.1 |
| Sugar Solution | 12 | 1.1 |
| Whole Milk | 14.5 | 1.02 |
| 2% Milk | 14 | 1.04 |

5. Because a hydrometer measures relative densities, ask students to predict the order in which water, corn syrup, and cooking oil will arrange themselves if poured together into a tall narrow container like a 100 mL graduated cylinder. [bottom layer, corn syrup; middle layer, water; top layer, cooking oil] Use a test tube or 100 mL graduated cylinder to demonstrate this effect for students. The middle water level can be colored by placing a single drop of food coloring on the surface of the cooking oil. Food coloring, being more dense than cooking oil, will sink to the bottom of the cooking oil into the water. Over time, the food coloring will evenly color the middle layer.

## Extensions

1. Students can use a hydrometer to estimate how much sugar is in soft drinks. Have students do the activity *Sugar Highs* in Volume X, No. 10, of *AIMS®*.

2. Have students check their hydrometer results with a scale or balance. Tell them to measure the weight or mass of a specified volume of water and then the same volume of Liquid *X*. Instruct them to calculate the ratio of the weight or mass of liquid X to the weight or mass of the same volume of water. This ratio is the specific gravity of Liquid X. Usually this method is more accurate than the hydrometer, but the hydrometer is far easier and quicker to use.

\*   Reprinted with permission from *Principles and Standards for School Mathematics*, 2000 by the National Council of Teachers of Mathematics. All rights reserved.

# Hippo Hydrometer Scales

| 0 | 5 | 10 | 15 | 20 | 25 | 30 | | 0 | 5 | 10 | 15 | 20 | 25 | 30 |

| 0 | 5 | 10 | 15 | 20 | 25 | 30 | | 0 | 5 | 10 | 15 | 20 | 25 | 30 |

| 0 | 5 | 10 | 15 | 20 | 25 | 30 | | 0 | 5 | 10 | 15 | 20 | 25 | 30 |

| 0 | 5 | 10 | 15 | 20 | 25 | 30 | | 0 | 5 | 10 | 15 | 20 | 25 | 30 |

| 0 | 5 | 10 | 15 | 20 | 25 | 30 | | 0 | 5 | 10 | 15 | 20 | 25 | 30 |

| 0 | 5 | 10 | 15 | 20 | 25 | 30 | | 0 | 5 | 10 | 15 | 20 | 25 | 30 |

| 0 | 5 | 10 | 15 | 20 | 25 | 30 | | 0 | 5 | 10 | 15 | 20 | 25 | 30 |

| 0 | 5 | 10 | 15 | 20 | 25 | 30 | | 0 | 5 | 10 | 15 | 20 | 25 | 30 |

| 0 | 5 | 10 | 15 | 20 | 25 | 30 | | 0 | 5 | 10 | 15 | 20 | 25 | 30 |

| 0 | 5 | 10 | 15 | 20 | 25 | 30 | | 0 | 5 | 10 | 15 | 20 | 25 | 30 |

| 0 | 5 | 10 | 15 | 20 | 25 | 30 | | 0 | 5 | 10 | 15 | 20 | 25 | 30 |

| 0 | 5 | 10 | 15 | 20 | 25 | 30 | | 0 | 5 | 10 | 15 | 20 | 25 | 30 |

| 0 | 5 | 10 | 15 | 20 | 25 | 30 | | 0 | 5 | 10 | 15 | 20 | 25 | 30 |

| 0 | 5 | 10 | 15 | 20 | 25 | 30 | | 0 | 5 | 10 | 15 | 20 | 25 | 30 |

| 0 | 5 | 10 | 15 | 20 | 25 | 30 | | 0 | 5 | 10 | 15 | 20 | 25 | 30 |

# Making A Hydrometer

1. Cut the clear plastic drinking straw so that it is 9 cm long.

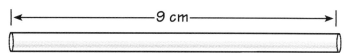

2. Roll the piece of clay into a ball. Insert one end of the straw into the clay.

clay ball ———

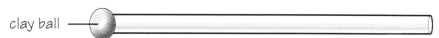

3. Trim off the extra clay with your fingers. The clay should form a plug in the end of the straw.

clay plug ———

4. Cut out a scale piece. Fold in its sides to make a triangular shape.

5. Tilt the straw and drop three BBs into the straw.

6. Slide the scale piece into the straw. The scale piece should slide easily in and out of the straw. Allow 1 cm of the scale piece to extend from the end of the straw.

sliding scale

7. Place the hydrometer in a clear glass of water. Slide the scale piece up or down until the "15" mark on the scale is at the water level. Your hydrometer is now calibrated to measure whether a different liquid is more dense or less dense than water.

8. You must constantly check the calibration of your hydrometer by placing it in water and observing that the "15" line is still at the water level. Carefully wipe the hydrometer dry each time you check its calibration.

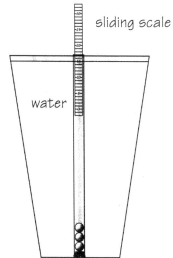

sliding scale

water

# Hippo Hydrometer Record

1. The specific gravity of water is 1.0. Look at the Hippo Hydrometer Graph and see that the point that represents the specific gravity of water has been located and labeled.

2. The specific gravity of Karo® corn syrup is 1.3. Place your Hippo Hydrometer in Karo® corn syrup and verify that it reads 6 units on the scale. On the graph, locate and label the point for Karo® corn syrup.

3. The specific gravity of Wesson® cooking oil is 0.9. Place your Hippo Hydrometer in Wesson® cooking oil and check that it reads 18 units on the scale. On the graph, locate and label the point for Wesson® cooking oil.

4. Draw the straight line through the three points on the graph.

5. Place the hydrometer in the saltwater solution. Read and record the number of scale units from the hydrometer. Locate the number of scale unit on the horizontal axis of the graph. Move straight up to the line. Move horizontally to the left to the vertical Specific Gravity axis. Read the value of the specific gravity from the axis and record this value in the Record Chart.

6. Repeat these steps to find the specific gravity of each of the other liquids.

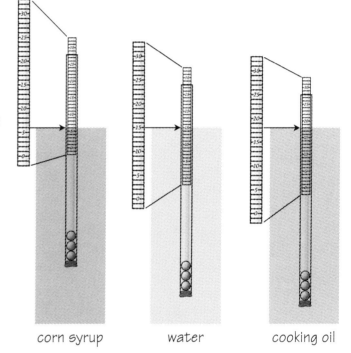

corn syrup          water          cooking oil

| Record Chart | | |
|---|---|---|
| Liquid | Hydrometer Scale Units | Specific Gravity |
| Water | | |
| Corn Syrup | | |
| Cooking Oil | | |
| Salt Water | | |
| Sugar Water | | |
| Whole Milk | | |
| 2% Milk | | |

# Hippo Hydrometer Graph

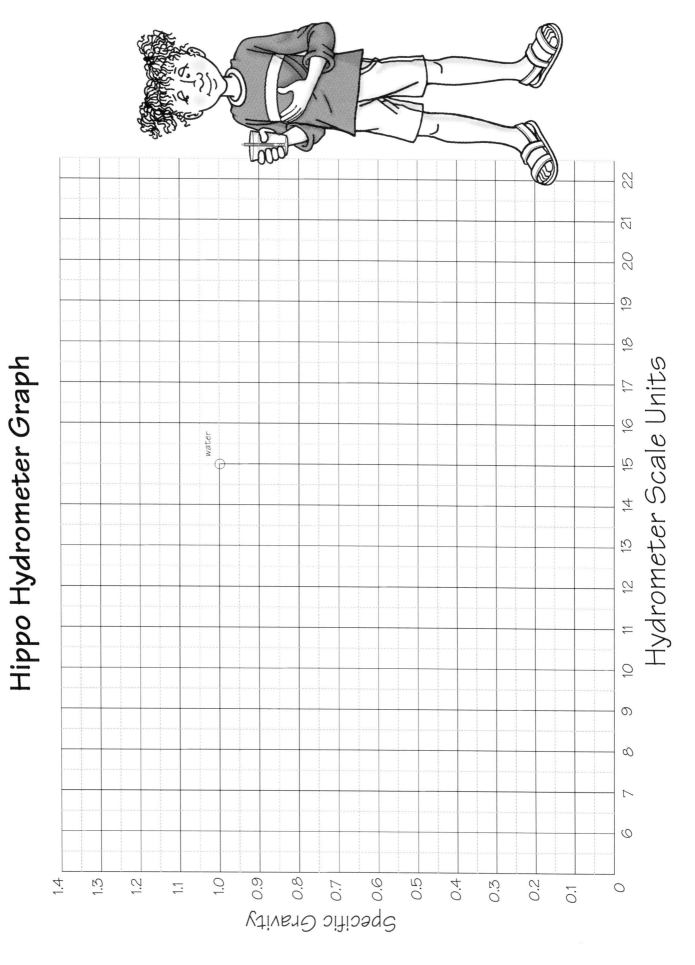

water

Specific Gravity

Hydrometer Scale Units

# Hydrometer Applications

A car mechanic uses a hydrometer to test a car battery because the specific gravity of a car battery's fluid is a measure of whether the battery is okay or near failure. When the acid solution in a car battery has a specific gravity of 1.30, the battery is okay. When the specific gravity drops to about 1.15, the battery is no longer working. Students should not use the Hippo Hydrometer to test the fluid in car batteries or any other fluid that may be strongly acidic or alkaline.

Modern, inexpensive hydrometers such as the type used by car mechanics are made with several small plastic balls inside a large eyedropper. The balls are different densities. When liquid is drawn into the dropper, the observer sees which balls float and which balls sink. This observation is compared with a chart that comes with the hydrometer to estimate the specific gravity of the liquid. *Hippo Hydrometer* teaches how to make a different type of hydrometer that does not require plastic balls of different densities.

A hydrometer may also be used in food and chemical processes to check a liquid that is being processed. For example, when maple sap is being processed into maple syrup by boiling to evaporate water, a hydrometer can be used to measure the specific gravity, so the cooks know when to stop boiling. As water evaporates, the sugar concentration of the maple sap/syrup liquid increases, so the specific gravity increases. Students can also use a hydrometer to estimate how much sugar is in soft drinks (see "Sugar Highs," *AIMS®* Volume X, No. 10), but the fizz must first be eliminated because the bubbles of carbonation cause errors in the measurements.

A classroom application for the hydrometer is to predict whether the interface between two liquids will be Rayleigh-Taylor unstable. If the upper liquid is more dense than the lower one, Rayleigh-Taylor Instability (RTI) occurs. A hydrometer measures the relative density between two liquids so the observer can predict whether a horizontal interface between two liquids will be unstable. RTI can only tell you if the upper liquid is more dense, but a hydrometer can actually be used to measure the ratio of the densities of the upper and lower liquids, provided calibrations with known liquids are done carefully. If the upper liquid is less dense than the lower one, the horizontal interface between them is stable and the liquids are said to be stratified. Ripples that may occur at the interface just die away.

# A Density Puzzler

The density of light corn syrup (as determined in the *Hippo Hydrometer* activity) is 1.3 $g/cm^3$. The density of water is 1.0 $g/cm^3$. Water, being less dense than light corn syrup, should float on top of light corn syrup. To verify this, pour a small amount of light corn syrup into a plastic cup. Carefully and slowly, pour water down the side of the cup. The interface between the light corn syrup and the water is clearly seen.

light corn syrup

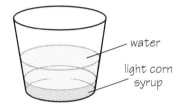
water
light corn syrup

Carefully and slowly, pour the water out of the cup, leaving the light corn syrup in the cup. Cut a one centimeter section from the end of a crayon.

1 cm
crayon

Half-fill a second cup with water. Place the crayon in the water. If the density of the crayon is greater than one $g/cm^3$, the crayon will sink to the bottom of the cup of water. Remove the crayon and dry it with a piece of paper towel.

Add more light corn syrup to the cup containing light corn syrup. Place the crayon in the cup containing the light corn syrup. The crayon, being less dense than light corn syrup, will float.

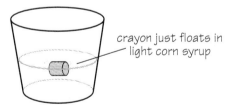
crayon just floats in light corn syrup

Question:   When enough water is added to the cup to cover the crayon, will the crayon:

    a.  remain at the same level in the light corn syrup,

    b.  float higher in the light corn syrup, or

    c.  float lower in the light corn syrup?

Make your prediction and then add water to the cup containing the corn syrup and the floating crayon to check the accuracy of your prediction.

79

# Open-tube Manometer

## Topic
Fluid pressure

## Key Question
How can air pressure and water pressure be indicated and measured?

## Focus
Students will construct a simple open-tube manometer and use it to indicate and measure water and air pressure.

## Guiding Documents
*Project 2061 Benchmark*
- *Read analog and digital meters on instruments used to make direct measurements of length, volume, weight, elapsed time, rates, and temperature, and choose appropriate units for reporting various magnitudes.*

*NRC Standard*
- *Use appropriate tools and techniques to gather, analyze, and interpret data.*

*NCTM Standards 2000\**
- *Represent, analyze, and generalize a variety of patterns with tables, graphs, words, and, when possible, symbolic rules*
- *Select and apply techniques and tools. Accurately find length, area, volume, and angle measures to appropriate levels of precision*
- *Recognize and apply mathematics in contexts outside of mathematics*

## Math
Measurement
    length
    area
    mass
    weight

## Science
Physical science
    force
        fluid pressure

## Integrated Processes
Observing
Collecting and recording data
Constructing

## Materials
*Per group:*
    6 plastic flex straws
    transparent tape
    cardboard box
    ball-point pen
    water container (example: two-liter bottle)
    petroleum jelly (small tube or jar)

## Background Information
The concept of *pressure* combines the concepts of *force* and *area*. Pressure is defined as *force* divided by *area*. The pressure can be viewed as the force acting on a single unit of area.

$$\text{Pressure} = \frac{\text{force}}{\text{area}}$$

The concept of force is most easily illustrated for a solid, but it also applies to liquids and gases. Consider a 5 cm x 5 cm x 5 cm cube sitting on a flat surface. The cube has a weight of 125 gram-force (gf). *Weight is a measure of the force of gravity pulling down* on the cube. The area of the face of the cube in contact with the surface is 25 square cm (5 cm x 5 cm).

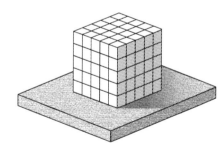

The pressure the cube exerts on the flat surface is equal to 125 gf/25 cm² or 5 gf/cm². If an index card is inserted between the top layer that is 5 cm x 5 cm x 1 cm high the second 1–cm–high layer, then only the top layer is pressing down on the card, so the pressure on the card is 25 gf/25 cm² or 1 gf/cm². The lower four layers, each 1 cm high, are not pressing down on the card so they do not add to the pressure. If a card is place between the second 1–cm–high layer and third layer, then the pressure on the card is 2 gf/cm² because the weight of two 1–cm–high layers is pressing down on the card. The pressure on the card increases as the card is placed lower from the top of the cube.

Now consider the cube as water within an aquarium with dimensions of 5 cm x 5 cm x 5 cm.

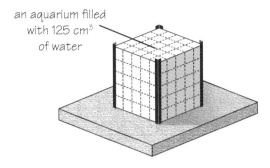

an aquarium filled with 125 cm³ of water

The force on the floor of the aquarium is 5 gf/cm², the same as it is for the solid cube. If an index card is placed horizontally in the aquarium 1 cm below the top surface, the pressure on the card is 1 gf/cm². If the card is placed horizontally 2 cm below the surface, the pressure is 2 gf/cm². The pressure on the card increases with depth.

To measure the pressure in fluids like air and water, we use a simple device called a open-tube manometer. It cannot measure the pressure caused by a solid but this activity will be concerned only with fluid pressure.

An open-tube manometer consists of a hollow tube bent into a U-shape, stood vertically, and filled with a liquid. Since both ends of the tube are open, atmospheric air pushes equally on the liquid surfaces and the liquid levels in both arms are at the same height.

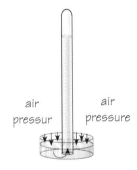

atmospheric pressure

equal levels

A        B

Increasing or decreasing the pressure on the surface of the liquid in one arm, but not the other, will cause the liquid level in the other arm to rise or fall. This can be demonstrated by connecting a short piece of tubing to one arm of the manometer and blowing gently into the tubing.

Blowing in the end of the tube increases the force acting on the surface A of the fluid which increases the pressure and drives the column of fluid downwards. Since the fluid is essentially incompressible, the fluid level in the other arm B must rise by an equal amount. The difference in levels A and B is a measure of pressure. A calibrated scale is added to the manometer to convert changes in the height (the difference in the levels of A and B) of the liquid to pressure units.

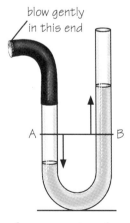

blow gently in this end

A        B

A *barometer* is a special type of manometer. A barometer is a *closed-tube* manometer. A simple barometer consists of a glass tube closed at one end and open at the other end.

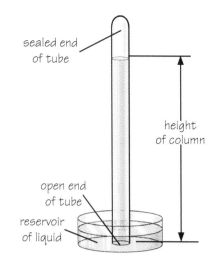

sealed end of tube

height of column

open end of tube

reservoir of liquid

The tube is filled with mercury and stands in a reservoir of mercury. (WARNING: mercury is a poisonous substance. Do not attempt to make a simple mercury-filled barometer.) The open end of the tube is below the surface of the reservoir. The surface of the reservoir is exposed to the atmosphere. The air pressure due to the weight of the atmosphere above the surface of the reservoir pushes down creating a pressure on the surface. This pressure is transmitted to the fluid in the tube which is free to move up the tube until its downward directed weight is balanced by the upward directed pressure.

air pressur        air pressure

Atmospheric pressure is capable of supporting a column of mercury 76 cm (about 30 inches) tall. Changes in atmospheric pressure are indicated by up and down changes in the height of the mercury column. Since mercury is approximately 13.3 times as dense as water, a 76 cm column of mercury is equivalent to a 1011 cm (76 cm x 13.3) or 34 foot column of water. (See *Trickle Triathlon* for an activity that explores the conditions under which atmospheric pressure will support a column of water in an inverted open-ended container.)

## Management
1. Organize students into groups of two or three.
2. Schedule one class period for constructing the manometer.
3. Have paper towels handy for cleaning up water spills.

4. Caution students not to blow in either arm of the water-filled open-tube manometer.
5. Keep a container of colored water and a few eye-droppers handy for re-leveling the manometers.

## Procedure

*Part One: Constructing an Open-tube Manometer*
Read and demonstrate to your students each step of this procedure.

1. Copy the *Pattern Page* and distribute one to each group.
2. Bend two flex straws into L-shapes. Have the longest section of each flex straw pointing up.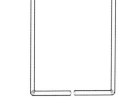
3. Use the tapered end of a ball-point pen or pencil to flare the end of one of the flex straws. Insert the pen into the straw and gently rotate it to produce the flared end.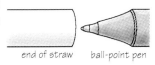

   end of straw     ball-point pen
4. Apply a film of of petroleum jelly to the end of the other flex straw and slide it into the flared straw. Wrap a short piece of transparent tape around the joint to keep it from separating.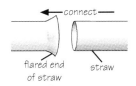

   connect

   flared end      straw
   of straw
5. Cut the *Open-tube Manometer* face from the *Pattern Page* and tape it to a cardboard box.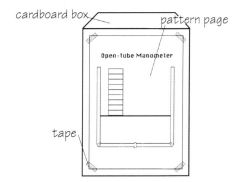

   cardboard box     pattern page

   Open-tube Manometer

   tape
6. Tape the U-shaped straws over the pictures of straws on the manometer face.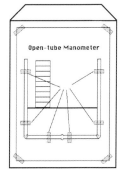

   Open-tube Manometer

7. Put a few drops of food coloring into a glass of water. Use an eyedropper to drop colored water into the left arm of the U-tube. Fill the straws until the water level on the left side coincides with the zero-mark on the scale.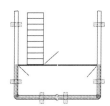

8. Starting from the long end, use a waterproof marker to mark one-centimeter divisions along one flex straw. This straw will be the pressure probe.

   one-centimeter
   divisions

9. Using the construction steps 2 and 3, connect the marked straw to three other flex straws.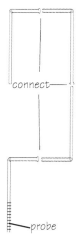

   connect

   probe

10. Insert the upper left end of the connected straws into the right arm of the manometer.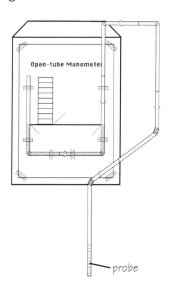

    Open-tube Manometer

    probe

*Part Two: Using the Open-tube Manometer*
1. Instruct one student per group to fill the water container to a level about two inches below the top. If the water level is at the top, the threads of the bottle's mouth obscure the reading of the probe.
2. Distribute the student page.

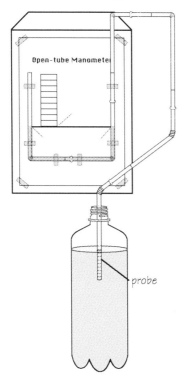

3. Tell the students to slowly lower the marked straw, keeping it as vertical as possible, into the water container. Ask them to observe the movement of the fluid level in the left arm of the manometer as they lower and raise the straw. After the students have had a few minutes to explore, ask them to answer the first question on the student page.
4. Tell the students to measure and record on the student page the pressure at one centimeter intervals to a depth of 10 centimeters.
5. Instruct the students to graph the data from the table.
6. Have the students draw the straight line through the plotted data points that they think best fits the data.
7. Tell the students to extend the line on the graph and then predict and record, from the graph, the pressure at depths of 15 and 20 centimeters.
8. Ask students to explain how they could check their predictions.

## Discussion
1. What relationship do you see between depth and pressure?

2. How do the data in your table show this relationship?

| Depth | 0 | 1 | 2 | 3 | 4 | 5 | 6 | 7 | 8 | 9 | 10 |
|---|---|---|---|---|---|---|---|---|---|---|---|
| Pressure | 0 | 1 | 2 | 3 | 4 | 5 | 6 | 7 | 8 | 9 | 10 |

3. How is the relationship shown in the graph?

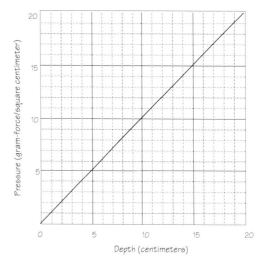

4. How could you confirm or reject the predictions you made? [extend the probe and test it]
5. How does this investigation relate to your experience swimming underwater?

*Middle-School and Secondary Students*
1. Inform students that water has a density of 1 gram per cubic centimeter. How does this value relate to the data in your table?
2. Express the relationship between *density* and *depth* in a liquid.
3. By looking at your graph and considering your response to the above question, write an equation that mathematically expresses the pressure in a liquid *as a function of* depth and the density of the liquid.
4. Explain how you could use this equation to determine the density of an unknown fluid. [In the linear equation that expresses the pressure in a liquid as a function of depth, density is the slope of the equation. The slope of the graph for a fluid denser than water will be greater than one. The slope of the graph for a fluid less dense than water will be less than one.]
5. Compare the pressures measured by the manometer with atmospheric pressure. The water pressure at a depth of 10 cm is 10 gf/cm². From the *Background Information*, we learned that atmospheric pressure at sea level will support a water column about 1000 cm high in a barometer. If we make the barometer from a large pipe 1 cm x 1 cm x 1000 cm high, closed at the top, then atmospheric pressure can hold the water in. The water pressure at the bottom of the pipe is 1000 gf/cm². That water pressure

83

equals the air pressure. So the air pressure around us (atmospheric pressure) is 100 times greater than the water pressure at a depth of 10 cm!

### Extensions

1. Collect several odd shaped plastic bottles. Fill each container with water and verify that the shape of the container does not affect pressure measurements.

2. *Measuring the air pressure in a toy balloon*
   An inflated toy balloon can be easily connected to the manometer. First, cut the tip off the rubber bulb from an eyedropper.

cut off tip

Insert a three-inch section of a plastic straw through the bulb. Wrap several layers of tape around the barrel of the rubber bulb. Test by slipping a toy balloon onto the bulb. Wrap the bulb until the balloon fits tight.

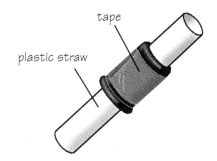

tape

plastic straw

Partially inflate the balloon, squeeze the end closed, and attach it the right arm of the manometer.

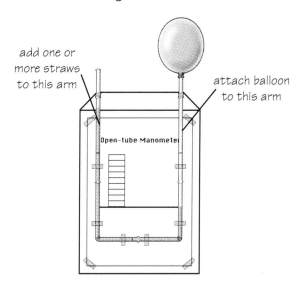

add one or more straws to this arm

attach balloon to this arm

Open-tube Manometer

Instruct a student to hold a sheet of paper over the end of the left arm of the manometer to deflect any liquid expelled from the straw if the air from the balloon is released too fast. Slowly, very slowly, release the air in the balloon into the manometer. If you release the air too quickly, it will eject all of the fluid from the left arm of the manometer.

* Reprinted with permission from *Principles and Standards for School Mathematics*, 2000 by the National Council of Teachers of Mathematics. All rights reserved.

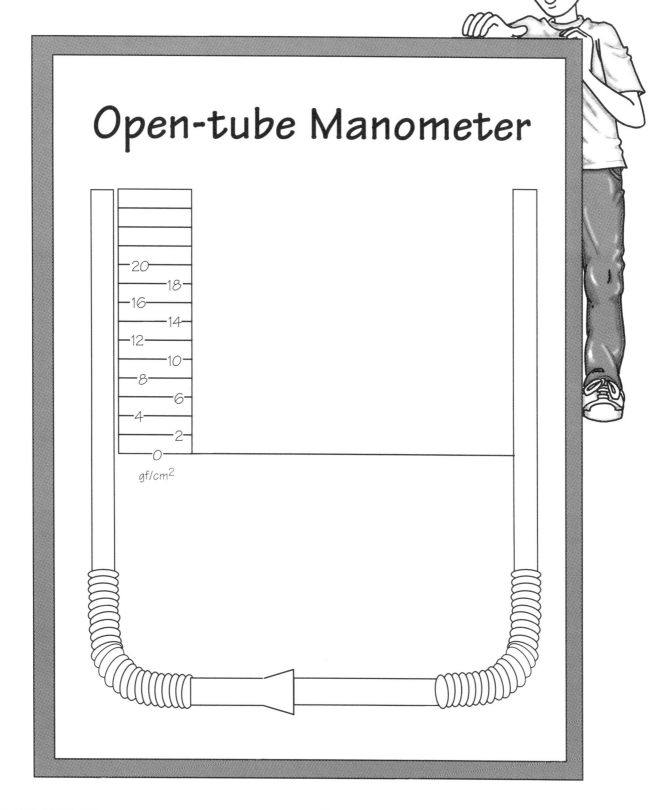

## Open-tube Manometer

# Open-tube Manometer

1. Describe in your own words the relationship between depth and pressure in a liquid.

2. Measure and record the pressure at one-centimeter intervals.

| Depth (D) cm | 0 | 1 | 2 | 3 | 4 | 5 | 6 | 7 | 8 | 9 | 10 |
|---|---|---|---|---|---|---|---|---|---|---|---|
| Pressure (P) gf/cm² | | | | | | | | | | | |

3. Graph the data in the table.

4. Draw a straight line through the points plotted on the graph.

5. Extend the line and predict the pressure at depths of 15 and 20 centimeters.

6. Explain how you could check your predictions.

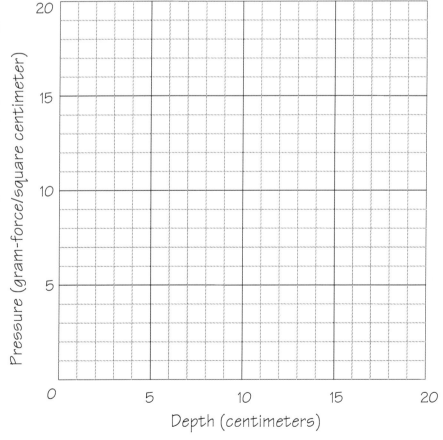

# Water Pressure Applications

An important application for water pressure is the engineering of a dam. A dam can be very deep. For example, the Grand Coulee Dam on the Columbia River in Washington state is 550 feet deep and the Hoover Dam on the Colorado River in Nevada is 730 feet deep.

The strength of a dam depends on the thickness of the dam's wall and the material of the wall. The strength of a dam must increase with water depth because water pressure increases with depth. Consequently the wall thickness increases with depth. The cross-section of a dam is approximately a trapezoid with the narrow part on top and the wider part on the bottom of the dam.

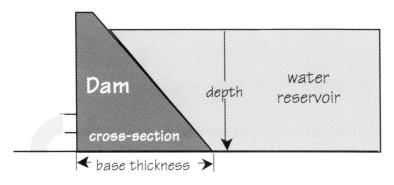

The base thickness of the Grand Coulee Dam is 500 feet (over $1\frac{1}{2}$ football fields!), and the Hoover Dam is 660 feet thick (over 2 football fields!).

Another application for water pressure is the limitations on a person who dives into a pool or lake. When a diver reaches a depth of 10 feet, the pressure increases from the pressure at the surface, 14.7 pounds per square inch (psi), to a pressure of 18 psi. This pressure change is nearly 30% of the air pressure at the surface and causes discomfort in a diver's ears. Greater depths cause problems with pressurized gas becoming dissolved in the diver's blood. If divers ascend too quickly, they get a condition called the bends.

# A Penny for Your Drops

## Topic
Surface tension

## Key Questions
*Part One*
How many drops of water will fit on a penny before it spills over?

*Part Two*
What variables affect the number of drops that will fit on a penny?

*Part Three*
How does adding soap to water affect the number of drops that can be placed on a penny?

## Foci
*Part One*
Students will explore surface tension by finding the number of drops of water that will fit on the head of a penny before it spills.

*Part Two*
Students will identify and control the variables affecting the outcome of this experiment.

*Part Three*
Students will explore the effect of soap on surface tension.

## Guiding Documents
*Project 2061 Benchmarks*
- *Results of similar scientific investigations seldom turn out exactly the same. Sometimes this is because of unexpected differences in the things being investigated, sometimes because of unrealized differences in the methods used or in the circumstances in which the investigation is carried out, and sometimes just because of uncertainties in observations. It is not always easy to tell which.*
- *Results of scientific investigations are seldom exactly the same, but if the differences are large, it is important to try and figure out why. One reason for following directions carefully and for keeping records on one's work is to provide information on what might have caused the differences.*
- *Keep records of their investigations and observations and not change the records later.*

*NRC Standards*
- *Use appropriate tools and techniques to gather, analyze, and interpret data.*

- *Develop descriptions, explanations, predictions, and models using evidence.*
- *Think critically and logically to make the relationships between evidence and explanations.*

*NCTM Standards 2000\**
- *Select and apply appropriate standard units and tools to measure length, area, volume, weight, time, temperature, and the size of angles*
- *Collect data using observations, surveys, and experiments*
- *Represent data using tables and graphs such as line plots, bar graphs, and line graphs*
- *Propose and justify conclusions and predictions that are based on data and design studies to further investigate the conclusion or predictions*

## Math
Counting
Statistics
    average

## Science
Physical science
    adhesion/cohesion
    surface tension

## Integrated Processes
Observing
Predicting
Collecting and recording data
Comparing and contrasting
Identifying and controlling variables
Interpreting data
Communicating

## Materials
*Part One*
    student sheet
    pennies, one per student
    eyedroppers, one per student
    small cups of water
    paper towels

*Part Two*
    student sheet
    newly-minted pennies, one per group
    eyedroppers, one per group
    small cups of water
    paper towels
    calculators, optional

*Part Three*
Same items as *Part Two*, plus:
   student sheet
   large container of soapy water

## Background Information

The surface of water has a tendency to act as if it is covered with a very thin net or skin. This phenomenon is called surface tension. (See page 11, *Surface Tension*, for more information.)

In this activity students see how many drops of water they can place on the surface of a penny. Because of surface tension and cohesion (attraction of like molecules for each other), a surprising amount of water can be placed on top of a penny. As drops are added, the water forms a dome-like shape that bulges above the edge of the penny. Surface tension keeps the water from spilling off and will support the bulging dome until the water piles so high that the force of gravity acting on the water becomes greater than the surface tension. At this point the water spills over the edge. Because the force of cohesion between the water molecules is much greater than the adhesion (attraction between unlike molecules) between the water and the copper in the penny, adding the last drop causes most of the water to flow right off the surface of the penny.

Several variables affect the amount of water that can be placed on a penny before it spills over. One set of variables involves the penny itself: its age, the side used, its condition, and any substances, like hand oils, that might be on its surface. A second set of variables includes how the experimenter performs the experiment: the technique used for dispensing the drops of water, the height the eyedropper is held above the penny, and the angle of the eyedropper.

Of these variables, the one that *appears* to make the most difference in the amount of water the penny holds (but doesn't necessarily) is the height of the eyedropper above the penny. If the dropper is too high, the surface tension can be broken prematurely by the force of the falling drops. When this happens, the amount of water the penny holds is reduced. However, if the dropper is held too close to the penny, something very different happens. The first few drops on the penny are a normal size, but as the dome of water builds up, subsequent drops touch the surface of the water below and are pulled out of the eyedropper before they are fully formed. In this case, students may count two to three times more drops on their pennies than the students who hold the eyedropper higher above the penny. A careful examination of the domes from table level will show that the amount of water on two pennies, one with twice the number of drops as the other, will be about the same. The amount of water *is not* significantly different, but the size of the drops varies greatly.

The last variable to be tested is the effect of adding soap to the water. This greatly reduces the surface tension of the water and therefore less soapy water will fit on a penny before spilling over. When using soapy water, the number of drops placed on a penny may not be substantially different from the number of drops for water, but the amount of water will be much smaller. This is evident when viewing the domes from table level. (Depending on the soap and eyedroppers used, you may get *more* drops of soapy water on a penny than plain water; however, as in the example given, these drops are much smaller and therefore the volume of water the penny holds is still *less*.)

## Management

*Part One*
1. The focus of this part of the activity is to demonstrate the need for carefully controlling variables. In this part, students work alone to see how many drops of water they can get on their pennies. This usually produces a wide range of results, typically 15-30 drops, or more. This is actually desirable because it gives students the incentive to repeat the experiment to produce more consistent results.

2. In this part, each student needs a penny and eyedropper. If you do not have enough eyedroppers to go around, students may take turns. Students also need small cups of water for filling their eyedroppers. These cups can be shared between several students. Paper towels should be placed under the pennies to prevent the water from going everywhere when it spills, and to detect clearly when the water dome collapses.

3. The discussion at the conclusion of this part is critical. This discussion should help students see the need for identifying and carefully controlling variables. As you facilitate this discussion, guide students' thinking in the appropriate directions without giving away the answers.

*Part Two*
1. The focus of the second part of the activity is to determine the variables that affect the results and to repeat the experiment in a controlled manner. In this part, students work in groups and try to produce more consistent results. Following are some of the experimental controls which should be implemented. Your students may think of more, but these, at least, are essential. Each group should have a newly-minted penny so that the age and condition of the penny is not a variable. All of the pennies should be either heads up or tails up. Pennies should always be completely dry before each trial begins. As the water is dropped from the eyedropper, students should be at a consistent distance from the penny (one centimeter is suggested). Eyedroppers should all be held at the same angle. The vertical position is recommended.

2. For this part, select eyedroppers for the groups that appear to be giving similar results. All eyedroppers are not the same, and differences among them may account for some of the disparate results. If you plan to follow this activity with *Measuring Drops on a Penny*, be sure to have groups somehow identify their eyedroppers so they can use the same ones in that activity.

3. Students should be familiar with the procedure for calculating average before beginning this activity. You may wish to make calculators available for this task.

*Part Three*
1. The focus of this part of the activity is to determine the effect of using soapy water instead of fresh water. This part is also done in groups in a controlled manner.

2. Make a stock solution of soapy water in a large container to make the results more consistent. A small amount of liquid dish washing soap is all that is needed to reduce the surface tension of a large amount of water. If you plan to do the activity *Measuring Drops on a Penny* with your class, save the soap solution to reuse in that activity. Groups should use the same eyedropper and the same penny in *Part Three* as they did in *Part Two*.

3. After finishing *Part Three*, the pennies and eyedroppers should be carefully washed to remove all the soap. Any remaining soap can "contaminate" results in future experiments.

**Procedure**
*Part One*
1. Ask students the first *Key Question*: "How many drops of water will fit on a penny before it spills over?" Have students record their guesses on the first student sheet.

2. Hand out the necessary materials to each student. Be sure that students have a level place on which to work.

3. Have students carefully put drops of water on their pennies until the water spills over. Each student will count the number of drops and record this information on the sheet. Be sure they understand that the final drop which causes the water to spill over is not counted in the total.

4. As students are dropping water onto their pennies, encourage them to carefully observe the water before it spills over by getting eye-level with the penny.

5. As students finish, have them come up to the board and record the number of drops on their pennies before filling in the rest of the sheet.

6. When all students have finished, discuss the class results. It is quite likely that there will be a large range in the data and students should try to determine some of the reasons for this. (See *Discussion, Part One*.)

7. Discuss ways to control some of the variables in this experiment.

*Part Two*
1. Divide students into groups of three to five and hand out the second student sheet. Ask the second *Key Question*: "What variables affect the number of drops that will fit on a penny?"

2. On the second student sheet, have students list reasons for the large differences in the results from *Part One* and describe their plan for getting more accurate results in *Part Two*.

3. Repeat the experiment, with each group member doing one trial. Emphasize that each student should follow the plan carefully so that consistent results are obtained.

4. Make sure students view their pennies and the domes of water on the pennies from table level before the water spills over. Have them sketch what this looks like in the space provided on the student sheet.

5. As groups finish collecting their data, have them write their results, including the group average, on the board.

6. Discuss the differences between the results in the two experiments and evaluate the effectiveness of the experimental controls implemented in *Part Two*. The range of results should be much narrower.

7. If groups get markedly different results, have them swap pennies and redo the experiment. If the results are still disparate, have them switch eyedroppers. Doing this should isolate an anomalous penny or eyedropper.

*Part Three*
1. Hand out the third student sheet and soapy water solution to each group.

2. Ask students the third *Key Question*: "How does adding soap to water affect the number of drops that can be placed on a penny?" Have them write down their guess on their student sheet.

3. Follow the same procedure for *Part Two* and close with a time of class discussion where students compare the results of all three sections and discuss the effect of soap on surface tension.

**Discussion**
*Part One*
1. How close was your guess to the actual number of drops you got on your penny?

2. Did the number of drops you got surprise you? Why or why not?

3. How did the water on your penny look before it spilled over? [The water forms a large "dome" before spilling over the edge.]

4. Did that surprise you? Why or why not?

5. Look at the different results on the board. Which is the largest? Which is the smallest? How much of a difference is that?

6. What are some possible explanations for these differences? [differences in the height from which the water was dropped, drops touching the water on the penny before they were fully formed, differences in the size of the drops, penny being heads up versus tails up, condition of the penny, etc.]

7. Is it likely that someone who got 40 drops on the penny had twice as much water on the penny as someone who got 20 drops? [No.] What might explain this discrepancy? [The size of the drops are not the same due to uncontrolled variables.]

8. What are some ways we could get more consistent results? [See *Management, Part Two,* number one.]

*Part Two*

1. What plan did you come up with to make your results more consistent?

2. How successful was your plan?

3. Look at the class results on the board. What is the difference this time between the smallest and largest numbers of drops?

4. How much of a change is that from the difference between the original results?

5. Based on the results for all of the groups, what is the average number of drops of water that will fit on a penny?

6. Why will so many drops of water fit on the head of a penny? [surface tension]

7. How do you know surface tension is at work? [You can see the water form a dome before it spills over.]

8. Where else have you seen or experienced surface tension? [Filling up a glass to above the rim without spilling the water, seeing bugs that can walk on the surface of water, etc.]

*Part Three*

1. What happened when you used soapy water on the penny? [Less soapy water fits on the penny because the surface tension of the water is reduced.]

2. If soap changes the size of the drops, how can you tell there is less soapy water on a penny than regular water? [When viewed at table level, the amount of soapy water on the penny is obviously less.]

3. Compare the results from *Part Two.* What differences do you see?

4. Based on the results of all of the groups, what is the average number of drops of soapy water that will fit on a penny? [The number of drops of soapy water could be less, the same, or greater depending on several variables. The *amount* of soapy water on the penny, however, will be much less.]

5. Is this number greater or less than the average for regular water?

6. How did the soapy water on the penny look before it spilled over? [The dome formed by soapy water is smaller than the dome formed by regular water.]

7. Why was the dome for the soapy water smaller? [The soapy water has less surface tension than the regular water and does not form as big of a dome before spilling over.]

8. What do you think is the reason for this? [Soap reduces the surface tension of water.]

**Extensions**

1. Repeat the experiment with other liquids such as rubbing alcohol or milk and compare the results. Which liquid has the greatest surface tension?

2. Try other coins and compare the results to the pennies.

* Reprinted with permission from *Principles and Standards for School Mathematics,* 2000 by the National Council of Teachers of Mathematics. All rights reserved.

# A Penny for Your Drops

## Part One

How many drops of water will fit on a penny before the water spills over?
Make a guess and record it here.

Place a paper towel on a level surface and lay a penny on top of the towel. Use an eyedropper to carefully put as many drops of water on the penny as you can. Count how many drops fit on the penny before the water spills. (Don't count the last drop.) Record your result here.

How close was your result to your guess?

How did the number of drops on your penny compare to the number of drops on other pennies?

How do you explain this?

What variables influenced the number of drops you could fit on a penny?

92

# A Penny for Your Drops

**Part Two**

In the first part of this activity, you discovered that a surprising amount of water will fit on a penny. This happens because of a property of liquids called *surface tension*. Surface tension makes the surface of water and other liquids act as if they have a thin "net" or "skin" stretched across them.

In this part of the activity your group is going to repeat the investigation with the goal of obtaining more accurate results.

Before repeating the investigation, list some of the possible reasons for the differences between individual results on the first part of this activity.

List the things your group can do to insure that the results are as accurate as possible.

Following the guidelines you have set up, see how many drops of water will fit on your group's penny. Take turns so that each person in your group does one trial. Watch each person carefully to be sure that they are following all of the guidelines. Be sure to view the water from table level before it spills over.

Sketch the water dome at the maximum number of drops.

| Trial # | Drops of Water |
|---------|----------------|
|         |                |
|         |                |
|         |                |
|         |                |
|         |                |
| Average |                |

How close are your results to those of other groups? Why did this happen?

## Part Three

# Penny for Your Drops

How does adding soap to water affect the number of drops that can be placed on a penny?

In the first parts of this activity you experimented with regular water drops on the face of a penny. In this part, you will explore what happens when soap is added to the water. How many drops of soapy water do you think will fit on your group's penny?

Following the same procedures and guidelines as before, see how many drops of soapy water will fit on the surface of your penny before it spills over. Record your group's results in the table to the right. (Be sure to view the soapy water from table level before it spills over.)

Sketch the water dome at the maximum number of drops.

| Trial # | Drops of Water |
|---------|----------------|
|         |                |
|         |                |
|         |                |
|         |                |
|         |                |
| Average |                |

Using the number of drops as the indicator, what difference is there between these results and the ones using regular water?

What difference is there between the amount of water and soapy water on your penny as indicated by your sketches?

How do you explain this difference?

# Measuring Drops on a Penny

## Topic
Measurement

## Key Questions
What is the mass of the average amount of water that will fit on the face of a penny?

What is the mass of the average amount of soapy water that will fit on the face of a penny?

## Focus
Students will determine the average amount of water, in grams, that will fit on the face of a penny before it spills over and then compare this to the mass of soapy water on a penny.

## Guiding Documents
*Project 2061 Benchmarks*
- *Measurements are always likely to give slightly different numbers, even when what is being measured stays the same.*
- *Comparisons of data from two groups should involve comparing both their middles and the spreads around them.*
- *Keep records of their investigations and observations and not change the records later.*
- *Organize information in simple tables and graphs and identify the relationships they reveal.*

*NRC Standards*
- *Use appropriate tools and techniques to gather, analyze, and interpret data.*
- *Think critically and logically to make the relationships between evidence and explanations.*
- *Use mathematics in all areas of scientific inquiry.*

*NCTM Standards 2000\**
- *Select and apply appropriate standard units and tools to measure length, area, volume, weight, time, temperature, and the size of angles*
- *Collect data using observations, surveys, and experiments*
- *Represent data using tables and graphs such as line plots, bar graphs, and line graphs*
- *Propose and justify conclusions and predictions that are based on data and design studies to further investigate the conclusion or predictions*

## Science
Physical science
   adhesion/cohesion
   surface tension

## Math
Measurement
   mass
Statistics and probability
   average (mean)
   range
Estimation
   rounding
Rational numbers
   decimals

## Integrated Processes
Observing
Collecting and recording data
Comparing and contrasting
Identifying and controlling variables
Interpreting data
Communicating
Relating
Generalizing

## Materials
*For each group:*
   paper towels
   eyedropper
   balance
   gram masses
   water
   soapy water (see *Management*)

*For each student:*
   student sheets
   calculator

## Background Information
After students have explored surface tension and its properties in *A Penny for Your Drops*, this activity helps them quantify the amount of water a penny will hold before the water spills. Doing this gives students a quantitative measure of the effect of surface tension. To determine the amounts of water their pennies hold, students find the average number of drops of water (from their eyedroppers) that have a mass of one gram. After finding how many drops there are in a

gram, students can use the data (numbers of drops they got on their pennies) from *A Penny for Your Drops* to calculate the mass of water their pennies held. Since a gram of water has a volume of about one milliliter or cubic centimeter, students can convert their mass data into volumes.

After doing this process for plain water, students will use the same procedure to find the average amount of soapy water that fits on a penny before it spills over. Doing this will help students quantify the effect soap has on the surface tension of water. Just a small amount of soap greatly reduces the surface tension of water. This reduction keeps soapy drops from getting as large as drops of plain water and thus there are many more soapy drops per gram than plain water drops. When this fact is combined with the results from the soapy water portion of *A Penny for Your Drops,* students calculate that their pennies hold much less soapy water than water—typically less than half as much.

## Management
1. This activity is designed to follow *A Penny for Your Drops* because it makes use of data collected in that activity. Students must complete that activity before beginning this one.
2. In contrast to *A Penny for Your Drops*, this activity utilizes more mathematics. Students should be familiar with how to calculate the average (mean) and the range of a set of data, as well as apply rounding techniques.
3. Because the numbers with which students will be dealing are likely to include decimals, calculators are recommended.
4. Students should work on this activity in the same groups that they were in for *A Penny for Your Drops* to maintain consistency with the results and techniques used. Groups should also use the same eyedroppers to keep the results consistent. However, all eyedroppers should be rinsed thoroughly before this activity to remove any soapy residue that could alter the results.
5. The second section of this activity has students use a solution of soapy water. To maintain consistency across all groups and with the results achieved from *A Penny for Your Drops,* the same solution should be used by all groups and in both activities. Different solutions can produce very different results, so consistency is important to insure that comparisons are valid.
6. Before students begin this activity, have a class discussion to talk about the techniques necessary to insure the most accurate results possible. These include, but are not limited to, making sure the balance is properly zeroed before beginning, drying out the tray completely between mass

readings, and making sure that a complete drop falls onto the balance each time.
7. After the activity is finished, it is important to remember that the soap used has *contaminated* the cups, pennies, and eyedroppers. *These items must be carefully rinsed and dried with clean paper towels to remove all the soap before they are used again for plain-water investigations.*

## Procedure
1. Hand out the student sheets and go over the procedure for the investigation. Before students begin, conduct the class discussion to set guidelines to insure the maximum consistency possible.
2. Have students get into their groups and distribute the appropriate materials for the first section. If necessary, instruct students on how to zero and read the balances.
3. Give all groups time to complete the first section and determine the number of drops of water in one, five, and ten grams.
4. When all groups have completed the first section, hand out the soapy water so that students can complete the second section.
5. After all students have had time to make the calculations and answer the questions on the fourth student sheet, close with a time of class discussion and sharing.

## Discussion
1. How similar were the number of drops per gram that you got based on a mass of one gram, five grams, and ten grams?
2. Was it different for soapy water and regular water? Explain.

3. Which measurement do you think is the most accurate? Why?
4. Based on your group's data, what was the average mass of plain water that would fit on a penny before spilling over?
5. Why do you think the values are different from group to group?
6. Based on your group's data, what was the average mass of soapy water that would fit on a penny before spilling over?
7. How do the average masses of soapy and plain water compare? [The average mass of soapy water that fits on a penny should be much less than that of the plain water.]
8. What does this difference in average masses tell you about the size of the drops? [The drops of soapy water are much smaller than those of plain water.]

9. How does this relate to surface tension and what you have already learned from *A Penny for Your Drops*. [Soap greatly reduces the surface tension of water, making the drops smaller and the amount of water that will stay on a penny less.]

### Extension
Have students place several drops of plain water and several drops of soapy water onto a paper towel from an eyedropper. When the rings of water have stopped spreading, trace around them and compare the size of the plain water drops to the soapy water drops. Older students may even be challenged to find the average area of a plain-water ring and a soapy-water ring.

*   Reprinted with permission from *Principles and Standards for School Mathematics*, 2000 by the National Council of Teachers of Mathematics. All rights reserved.

# Measuring Drops on a Penny

**Question:** How many drops of water from your eyedropper are there in one gram?

**Directions:**
1. Zero your balance with nothing in either pan.
2. Place a gram mass in one pan.
3. Hold the eyedropper over the opposite pan and count the number of drops of water it takes to balance the pans. Record this number in the table below.
4. Pour the water from the pan back into the cup and dry the pan completely.
5. Repeat this process again, and then do the same with a five-gram mass and a ten-gram mass. Record your results.
6. When you have completed the first part of the table, compute the values in the second part by dividing the number of drops by the number of grams. Round all results to the nearest tenth.

| # of Grams | # of Drops | | # of Drops per Gram |
|---|---|---|---|
| 1 | | ÷ 1 | |
| 1 | | ÷ 1 | |
| 5 | | ÷ 5 | |
| 5 | | ÷ 5 | |
| 10 | | ÷ 10 | |
| 10 | | ÷ 10 | |
| | | Average | |
| | | Range | |

# Measuring Drops on a Penny

**Question:** How many drops of soapy water are there in a gram?

**Directions:**
Use soapy water and follow the same procedure as you did on the first page. Record your results below and then calculate the number of drops of soapy water there are per gram.

| # of Grams | # of Drops | | # of Drops per Gram |
|:---:|:---:|:---:|:---:|
| 1 | | ÷ 1 | |
| 1 | | ÷ 1 | |
| 5 | | ÷ 5 | |
| 5 | | ÷ 5 | |
| 10 | | ÷ 10 | |
| 10 | | ÷ 10 | |
| | | Average | |
| | | Range | |

© 2001 AIMS Education Foundation

# Measuring Drops on a Penny

Using the information you have collected in this activity and in *A Penny for Your Drops*, it is possible to calculate the average mass of the water that collects on the surface of a penny before it spills over. To do this, take the average number of drops per penny and divide it by the average number of drops per gram to get the average number of grams of water. Show your work below.

**Plain water**

Average number of drops on a penny: _____

Average number of drops per gram: _____

Average number of grams of water on a penny: _____

**Soapy water**

Average number of drops on a penny: _____

Average number of drops per gram: _____

Average number of grams of water on a penny: _____

What do the data tell you about the effect of soap on the amount of water that will fit on a penny?

How is this related to surface tension?

# Measuring Drops on a Penny

1. How similar were the number of drops per gram when you found the amount of water in one gram, five grams, and ten grams of plain water? ...of soapy water?

2. Which measurement do you think is the most accurate? Why?

3. How do the average masses of plain and soapy water that will fit on a penny compare?

4. Does this surprise you? Why or why not?

5. What does the difference between the average masses tell you about the size of the drops?

6. How does this relate to surface tension?

# Pennies in a Cup

**Topic**
Surface tension

**Key Question**
How many pennies can you put in a cup filled to the brim with water before it spills over?

**Focus**
Students will explore the amazing property of surface tension.

**Guiding Documents**
*Project 2061 Benchmarks*
- *Use numerical data in describing and comparing objects and events.*
- *Organize information in simple tables and graphs and identify relationships they reveal.*

*NCTM Standards 2000\**
- *Collect data using observations, surveys, and experiments*
- *Represent data using tables and graphs such as line plots, bar graphs, and line graphs*
- *Select and apply appropriate standard units and tools to measure length, area, volume, weight, time, temperature, and the size of angles*

**Math**
Measuring
Counting

**Science**
Physical science
  surface tension
  cohesion
  adhesion

**Integrated Processes**
Observing
Identifying and controlling variables
Comparing and contrasting
Collecting and recording data
Interpreting data
Applying

**Materials**
Wide-rimmed, nine-ounce, transparent plastic cups
Paper towels
Large supply of pennies (see *Management*)

**Background Information**
Surface tension acts in the surface of a liquid and tends to minimize the area of that surface. All liquids possess surface tension in varying degrees, but water has the highest surface tension of any common liquid. Surface tension is caused by the physical properties of the molecules in a liquid. These molecules exhibit cohesion, an attractive force between like molecules due to unbalanced electrical charges. Cohesion keeps liquids together and varies in strength depending on the liquid. When liquids are in a container like a cup, the molecules beneath the surface are attracted to each other by cohesion. This attraction works equally in all directions. Those molecules on the surface, however, are only being attracted by the molecules to the side and below the surface, not above. This unbalanced attractive force makes the liquid act as if it has a thin skin or membrane on the surface.

In this activity, surface tension allows the water to bulge above the rim when pennies are carefully dropped into the cup. Amazingly, a cup of water filled level with the rim can accommodate a large number of pennies because of surface tension—about 65-75 pennies can be placed in a nine-ounce, wide-rimmed plastic cup. Seventy pennies displace about 25 mL of water, which is almost 10 percent of the volume of the nine-ounce (265 mL) cup. Thus, the bulge produced above the rim of the cup when the pennies displace the water has a volume of about 25 mL.

Another related concept dealt with in this activity is displacement. Objects, such as pennies, that sink in a liquid displace, or push out of the way, a volume of water equal to the object's volume. (Things that float in a liquid displace a volume of liquid with a weight equal to the weight of the object—this is known as Archimedes' Principle.)

**Management**
1. This activity is designed to be done before *More Pennies in a Cup* since it sets the stage for that follow-up activity. The two activities can be done on the same day or different days.

2. Students should work in pairs or small groups when doing this activity.
3. Because water is involved, you need to have a source of water and plenty of paper towels.
4. Students need a stable, level surface on which to work.
5. A large number of pennies is needed for this activity. Each cup can hold about 70 pennies before it spills over—use this number to calculate the approximate number of pennies needed. You can get rolls of pennies from the bank or ask a student to bring in a penny jar.
6. If you want your students to accurately measure the volume of water in the bulge produced by the pennies, you will need eyedroppers and graduated cylinders. An alternative is to use an oral syringe which can be purchased from a drug store, from veterinarians, or from animal supply stores that cater to livestock owners.

## Procedure

1. Hand out the student sheet, two plastic cups, some paper towels, and a handful of pennies to each group.
2. Explain the activity to the class. Have students fill their cups about two-thirds full of water.
3. Have students place one of the cups on a dry paper towel and then fill it using the water from the other cup. The cup on the towel should be filled level with the rim, but no higher. Students will need to sight the cup from rim level in order to do this.
4. Tell students to place one penny at a time, edgewise, into the water. This should be done carefully so that the cup doesn't spill prematurely. Students should try to perfect their technique to get close to the maximum number possible. They should observe the cup during this process from rim level.
5. Have students continue to add pennies while keeping track of the number added. Tell students to stop adding pennies when the cup spills over the first time and wets the paper towel. Have them record the number of pennies on the student sheet. Remind them not to count the last one.
6. Have students draw a picture of their observations of the cup from rim level.
7. Share the results of each group in a whole class session and write them on the chalkboard. (The results could be recorded in the form of a class histogram.) Discuss why the results are not all the same.

8. Discuss techniques that might allow more pennies to be added to the cup.
9. After the class discussion, have students write their conclusions at the bottom of the sheet.

## Discussion

1. How close were your predictions and results?
2. What allowed so many pennies to be placed in the cup before it overflowed? [The surface tension of the water allowed it to be displaced above the rim of the cup.]
3. Why weren't the results all the same? [There are several possible reasons: technique of putting in the pennies, starting water level, steadiness of the table supporting the cup.]
4. What techniques might allow you to maximize the number of pennies? [make sure the cup is filled exactly to the rim and not above it, put pennies in very carefully (hold pennies edgewise and hang on to them until they break the water's surface before letting go) so ripples don't form, make sure the table is not bumped, etc.]
5. How much water do you think is in the bulge above the rim when the maximum number of pennies is added? [It is equal to the volume of the pennies. How could you measure this volume? [Use an eyedropper to remove the bulge and place it in a graduated cylinder; put an equal number of pennies in a graduated cylinder filled with a known amount of water and see how much water is displaced, use an oral syringe marked in mL to draw off the excess water.]
6. What extensions can you think of to explore?

## Extensions

1. Test various containers to see how the size of the opening affects the number of pennies held. For example, try a two-liter soda bottle. [About four pennies cause it to spill.]
2. Test containers that have the same sized openings but are made of different materials (e.g., glass, ceramic, or plastic) to see the effect of the material on the number of pennies the container will hold.
3. Find the volume of the water in the bulge when the maximum number of pennies has been added.

* Reprinted with permission from *Principles and Standards for School Mathematics*, 2000 by the National Council of Teachers of Mathematics. All rights reserved.

# Pennies in a Cup

How many pennies can you put in a cup filled to the brim with water before it spills over?

Make your prediction: _____ pennies

Work with a partner. You will need two plastic cups, a handful of pennies, some paper towels, and a level place to work.

Fill both cups about two-thirds full of water. Place one cup on a dry paper towel and use the water in the second cup to carefully fill the first cup until its water level is exactly even with the rim. (You will need to get down at rim level to check this.)

Carefully add one penny at a time to the cup while keeping track of the number. Try to get as many pennies in the cup as possible. Observe what happens to the surface of the water as you add pennies by sighting the cup at rim level. Keep going until water spills over the rim and the paper towel gets wet. How many pennies did your cup hold? (Do not count the last penny.) _____ pennies

Carefully observe your cup from rim level and in the space below draw a picture of what you see just before it spills over.

What techniques might allow you to get more pennies in the cup?

Share your results with others in the class. Write about your findings in the space below.

# MORE Pennies in a Cup

## Topic
Surface tension

## Key Question
How do the surface tensions of water and soapy water compare?

## Focus
Students will explore the surface tension of water as it compares to the surface tension of soapy water.

## Guiding Documents
*Project 2061 Benchmarks*
- *Seeing how a model works after changes are made to it may suggest how the real thing would work if the same were done to it.*
- *Organize information in simple tables and graphs and identify relationships they reveal.*

*NCTM Standards 2000\**
- *Collect data using observations, surveys, and experiments*
- *Represent data using tables and graphs such as line plots, bar graphs, and line graphs*
- *Select and apply appropriate standard units and tools to measure length, area, volume, weight, time, temperature, and the size of angles*

## Math
Counting
Measuring
    volume
    surface area
    mass
Ratios
Statistics and probability
    mean
    range

## Science
Physical science
    surface tension
    cohesion
    adhesion

## Integrated Processes
Observing
Identifying and controlling variables
Comparing and contrasting
Collecting and recording data
Interpreting data
Applying

## Materials
Plastic cups (wide-rimmed, nine ounce), two per group
Paper towels
Large supply of pennies
Eyedroppers
Liquid dish detergent

## Background Information
See *Pennies in a Cup* for background information dealing with displacement and surface tension.

When soap is added to water, it greatly reduces the water's surface tension. The process causing this reduction is a complex one which requires looking at what happens at the molecular level. Soap molecules are long hydrocarbon chains. At one end of the chain is a *hydrophilic* (literally—water loving) head which is composed of a special configuration of atoms. These atoms are attracted to water. At the other end of the molecule is a waxy *hydrophobic* (literally—water fearing) tail composed of atoms which repel water molecules, but attract dirt and grease. When a drop of liquid soap is added to water, it very quickly spreads across the surface of the water. (This is evidenced in the classic demonstration where pepper is sprinkled on a water-filled pie pan and then a drop of detergent is added to the center—the soap film shoots across the surface of the water carrying the pepper with it.) As the soap film rapidly moves across the water, the hydrophilic heads of the soap molecules penetrate the water's surface while the hydrophobic tails stick up above the surface. As the soap molecules do this, they squeeze between water molecules at the surface. This increased space between the surface water molecules decreases the attractive force (cohesion) between them and therefore significantly reduces the surface tension of the water.

## Management
1. This activity is designed as a follow-up to *Pennies in a Cup*. It is divided into two parts: an experiment using water and an experiment using soapy water. If students do not remember the methods and procedures used in *Pennies in a Cup*, a review will be necessary before they attempt *More Pennies in a Cup*.
2. Each group will need two plastic cups, a generous supply of paper towels, 80-100 pennies, and an eyedropper for the first part of the experiment. In the second part, all materials remain the same except for the addition of a few drops of soap to each group's water. Use a good quality liquid dish soap.

3. When groups are putting the soap in their water, be sure to emphasize that *very little soap* is needed to produce the desired effect. Two or three drops is the most any group should put in their cup. The more soap a group uses, the more suds and bubbles will be produced, making it more difficult for them to achieve accurate results. In addition, it is important to note that once soap is added to the water, it will contaminate the cups, pennies, and eyedroppers. *These items must be carefully rinsed and dried with clean paper towels to remove all the soap before they are used again for plain-water experiments.*

4. Once they collect their data, students are asked to calculate the average number of pennies that could be placed in their cup across five trials. They are also asked to determine the range of their results. If students are not familiar with how to calculate these two values, review these procedures before they begin.

## Procedure

*Part One*

1. Have students get into groups of no more than four and hand out the necessary materials for the first part to each group.

2. Remind students of the experimental procedure that they will need to use for each trial. If necessary, refer to the first student sheet from *Pennies in a Cup*.

3. Review the methods developed in *Pennies in a Cup* for maximizing the number of pennies which can be placed in a cup. (Drop the pennies edgewise, place the pennies partly in the water before letting go, don't bump the table, etc.)

4. Remind students that the wetness of the paper towel is the sole criterion for SPILL, even though the dome persists.

5. Hand out the first student sheet and allow groups sufficient time to do five trials with water and calculate the average and range.

6. Have a brief time of class discussion in which groups share their data and compare results.

*Part Two*

1. Have each group add a couple drops of soap to their cup of water and have them conduct their five trials with soapy water. Remind students to remove all suds and bubbles from the surface of the water before adding any pennies.

2. When all groups have completed the five trials, have them share data from the second part and compare results.

3. Hand out the second student sheet and allow students sufficient time to answer all of the questions.

4. Close with a class discussion where students draw conclusions about the effect of soap on the surface tension of water.

## Discussion

1. What was the average number of pennies that your group could fit in the cup of water before it spilled over?

2. What was the average number of pennies for soapy water?

3. How do these numbers compare?

4. How do the results that different groups arrived at compare?

5. What factors could account for the differences? [different initial water levels, differences in how pennies were dropped into the water, etc.]

6. Based on your experimental results, what can you conclude about the effect of soap on the surface tension of water? [It reduces the surface tension by about half.]

## Extensions

1. Have students compare the surface tension of water to other liquids such as rubbing alcohol, mouthwash, or various fruit juices.

2. Have students experiment with different amounts of soap in the water to determine what effect, if any, the amount of soap has on surface tension.

3. Once a cup and pennies get soap "contamination," they cannot be re-used for plain-water experiments without considerable effort. This might lead to an extension related to ecology where students learn to "decontaminate" surfaces.

* Reprinted with permission from *Principles and Standards for School Mathematics*, 2000 by the National Council of Teachers of Mathematics. All rights reserved.

# MORE Pennies in a Cup

In *Pennies in a Cup* you discovered that surface tension allowed a large number of pennies to be placed into a cup of water before it overflowed. Using methods which will maximize your results, try the experiment five more times to determine an average result. Record your results in the table below, including the range. (The largest result minus the smallest result is the range.)

## Water

Number of Pennies in the Cup

| | | |
|---|---|---|
| Trial 1 | | |
| Trial 2 | | |
| Trial 3 | | |
| Trial 4 | | |
| Trial 5 | | Range |
| Average | | |

Now that you have experimented with the surface tension of water, you will explore the effects of soap on surface tension. Place a few drops of soap into your cup of water to create a soapy mixture. Repeat the procedure you used above and record your results in the table below. Be sure to get rid of any suds or bubbles which collect on the surface of the water before you drop in your pennies.

## Soapy Water

Number of Pennies in the Cup

| | | |
|---|---|---|
| Trial 1 | | |
| Trial 2 | | |
| Trial 3 | | |
| Trial 4 | | |
| Trial 5 | | Range |
| Average | | |

# MORE Pennies in a Cup

When you have completed both parts of the investigation, answer the questions below.

1. What was the average number of pennies you were able to get into a full cup of water? ...the range?

2. How did your average compare to the results reached by other groups? Did your ranges overlap?

3. What was the average number of pennies you were able to get into a full cup of soapy water? ...the range?

4. How did your average for soapy water compare to the results reached by other groups? Did your ranges overlap?

5. Based on your results, what can you conclude about the effect of soap on the surface tension of water?

# Delicate Diver

## Topic
Pressure in a liquid

## Key Question
How can an underwater creature control its density and buoyancy?

## Focus
Students will make a Cartesian Diver using an eyedropper and a two-liter, clear plastic, water-filled bottle. Students will observe how the interplay between pressure and density affects buoyancy.

## Guiding Documents
*Project 2061 Benchmarks*
- *In the absence of retarding forces such as friction, an object will keep its direction of motion and its speed. Whenever an object is seen to speed up, slow down, or change direction, it can be assumed that an unbalanced force is acting on it. [ed. Newton's first law of motion.]*
- *Things near the earth fall to the ground unless something holds them up.*

*NRC Standard*
- *The position of an object can be described by locating it relative to another object or the background.*

*NCTM Standard 2000\**
- *Use common benchmarks to select appropriate methods for estimating measurements*

## Science
Physical science
  density
  pressure

## Integrated Processes
Observing
Comparing and contrasting
Collecting and recording data
Identifying and controlling variables

## Materials
Eyedropper
Two-liter plastic bottle with cap
Food coloring
Overhead transparencies, optional

## Background Information
A Cartesian Diver is a simple "underwater creature." It usually consists of a hollow, cylindrical-shaped object that is open at one end. The open end is weighted so that the cylinder floats vertically, open-end down, when immersed in water. Our diver is an eyedropper. The diver is placed in a water-filled container that can be slightly pressurized. One method for applying pressure is to fill the container to the brim, cover the opening with a flexible membrane and then apply a downward pressure to the membrane. The clear container may be glass or plastic. Another method of applying pressure is to fill a plastic container nearly to the top and seal it with its cap. Squeeze the bottle to apply pressure to the water. Both methods apply pressure to all of the water within the container.

When pressure is applied, a small amount of water flows through the opening at the bottom of the diver. This occurs because the air trapped within the dropper is compressed by the applied pressure but the water is not compressed. That is, in response to the pressure my hand applies, water does not change its volume but air does. When I apply pressure to the container, that pressure compresses the air trapped within the diver. When a sufficient amount of water is forced into the diver, the diver sinks to the bottom of the two-liter bottle because the density of the diver increases and it's no longer buoyant. Observing the water level within the diver is essential to predicting the diver's responses.

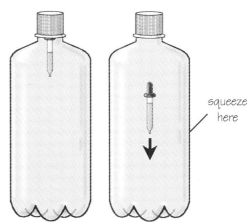

squeeze here

When the applied pressure on the container is released, the air within the diver expands by forcing water out of the diver. This action reduces the density of the diver. When enough water is expelled from the diver, the diver's density decreases below water density, the diver becomes buoyant and floats to the top. Again, observing the water level within the diver is a key diagnostic for predicting whether the diver will sink or float. Careful application of pressure can cause the diver to become "neutrally buoyant" so it rests near the center of the container.

The diver's position is determined by a delicate balance of two forces acting vertically on the diver. Gravity is forcing the diver downward. Buoyancy is forcing the diver upward. When the bottle is squeezed, it compresses the air within the diver, so the density of the diver increases. The diver sinks because the buoyant force has become less than the gravitational force. When the applied pressure is released, air within the diver expels water, so the diver's density decreases. When sufficient water leaves, the buoyant force exceeds gravity so the diver floats. This delicate balance is controlled by the density of the diver, which can be monitored by the water level within the dropper.

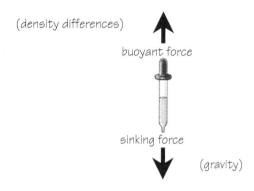

(density differences)

buoyant force

sinking force

(gravity)

Is the underwater creature known as a Cartesian Diver more like a fish or a submarine? That's debatable. Some say a submarine for the following reasons: The diver consists of three parts:

• the dropper and bulb,
• air space within the dropper and bulb, and
• the water within the dropper.

The volume of the diver remains the same whether the diver is floating or sinking. Diver density is lower when floating because the diver's mass is less. This is because a greater portion of the diver's volume is occupied by air than when the diver sinks. This viewpoint says that the diver works on the same principle as a submarine: Submarine volume is constant and it changes its mass to control its density. The mass increases and decreases by taking on water and later expelling it. Constant volume and controllable mass.

Another view of the diver is that the water in the dropper is not part of the diver. This view says that the diver's mass is constant and it changes density by changing volume. The volume changes when the trapped air is compressed or expands. This method is how a fish controls its depth. Its mass remains constant but its swim bladder regulates its volume. It has constant mass and controllable volume.

Viewing the Cartesian Diver as either a submarine or fish gives the same and correct result, but scientists and educators love to debate this point.

## Management

1. Students should work together in pairs.
2. Have containers and sponges available to catch water spills.
3. Experiment with the eyedroppers you intend to use to make sure you understand the parameters that make them work. Glass eyedroppers with a rubber bulb work best, but one-piece plastic eyedroppers can be weighted at the open end and made to work.

   If the eyedropper sinks when inserted into the bottle of water, the eyedropper is OVERFILLED. Retrieve the dropper by pouring water out of the two-liter bottle. Squeeze the eyedropper to expel some water. Refill the bottle and again place the eyedropper into the bottle. If it floats, put the cap on the bottle and proceed with the lesson.

   If the eyedropper fails to sink when the capped bottle is squeezed, then the eyedropper is UNDERFILLED. Open the bottle, remove the dropper, add more colored water to the eyedropper, put it back into the bottle, and cap the bottle. Squeeze the capped bottle and check that the eyedropper sinks. If not, it is still underfilled and needs more water.
4. Optional: Make transparencies of the *Bottle Background Scenes* page.

## Procedure

*Making a Cartesian Diver*

1. Instruct the students to fill the two-liter bottle to the brim with water.
2. Identify the parts of the eyedropper.

bulb          barrel          tip

3. Have the students cycle through a center containing several small cups of water that have been colored with yellow food coloring. Tell them to experiment to determine the *minimum* amount of water the eyedropper will hold in its barrel and sink to the bottom of the glass.

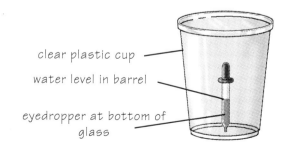

clear plastic cup

water level in barrel

eyedropper at bottom of glass

4. Tell the students to float the eyedropper, open-end down, in the neck of the two-liter bottle. Instruct

them to add any water necessary to bring the level back to the brim of the bottle.

5. Have them now screw the caps on the bottles.
6. If available, have students tape one of the background scenes to their bottle.

*Exploration*
1. Distribute the student page.
2. Tell the students to squeeze the sides of the bottle, observing, as they do so, the level of the yellow-colored water in the barrel of the eyedropper.
3. Instruct them to describe in their own words, on the student page, what they observed.
4. Ask students to observe and record on the eyedropper diagrams the colored water levels in the barrels of a floating eyedropper and an eyedropper that has sunk to the bottom of the bottle.

## Discussion

1. What did you observe? Sample observations are:
   - The eyedropper went down when the bottle was squeezed.
   - The eyedropper went up when the squeeze bottle was released.
   - The colored water in the barrel went up when the bottle was squeezed.
   - Colored water was pushed out the tip of the barrel when the bottle was squeezed.
   - Clear water entered the barrel of the eyedropper, through the tip, when the squeezed bottle was released.
   - The clear water in the tip soon mixed with the colored water.
   - The colored water stayed in the barrel of the eyedropper.
   - The eyedropper can be "stabilized" so that it neither floats at the top or rests on the bottom of the bottle.
2. Compare the basic structure of a submarine (a long tube filled with air) with the structure of an eyedropper. How is an eyedropper in a bottle is like a submarine? How is it different from a submarine? [A submarine contains large tanks that can be filled with water or emptied to make it sink or float.]

## Extensions

1. Buy a small plastic toy boat or experiment with any object that floats when empty of water but sinks when filled with water. Demonstrate this to the students and ask them to compare the floating-sinking boat to their floating-sinking eyedropper.

   Archimedes (287-212 B.C.) discovered that a body immersed in a fluid is "buoyed up" by a force equal to the weight of the displaced fluid.
2. This activity began by drawing a small amount of colored water into the barrel of an eyedropper. Just how does an eyedropper work?

The *Delicate Diver* shows the fundamentals of constructing and operating a Cartesian Diver. Squeezing a cylindrical bottle increases fluid pressure within the bottle, which increases the density of the diver by forcing water into the eyedropper. However, the *Reverse Diver* shows that squeezing a rectangular-shaped bottle in certain ways can decrease fluid pressure within the bottle and thereby *decrease* the diver's density. These two activities sharpen students' awareness of the importance of container geometry by showing that squeezing a plastic bottle can have opposite effects in changing volume and pressure, depending on the container shape.

---

# Bottle Background Scenes

1. Make a transparency of this page.
2. Cut out each of the two scenes.
3. Have students tape a scene to the back of their two-liter bottles.
4. Instead of using one of these scenes, students can design their own and draw it on the bottle using permanent marker. It can be colored with permanent marker.

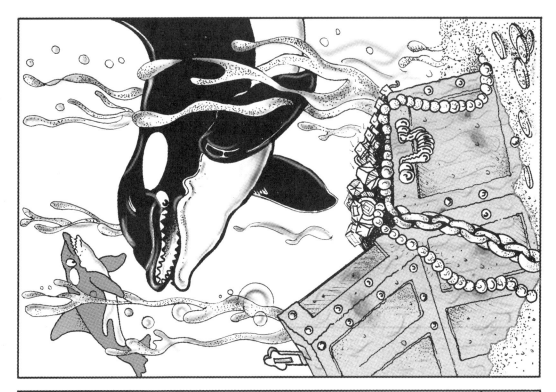

# Observations

Describe what you observe when you squeeze and release the sides of the bottle. If you think it will help, sketch an eyedropper in the bottle diagram.

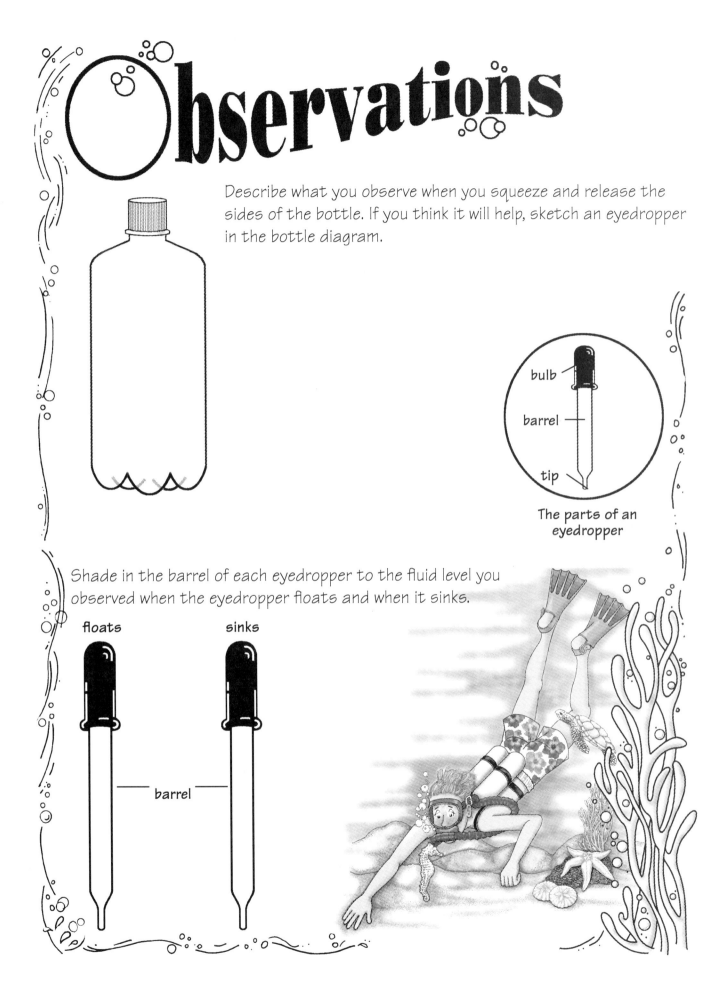

bulb

barrel

tip

The parts of an eyedropper

Shade in the barrel of each eyedropper to the fluid level you observed when the eyedropper floats and when it sinks.

floats

sinks

barrel

# The Diver's Dilemma: Submarine or Sea Animal?

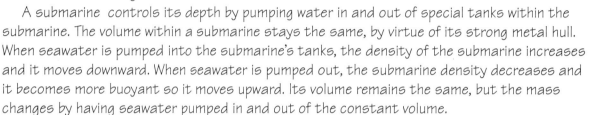

Explanations of the Cartesian Diver often lead to heated discussions among scientists and educators about the interplay of density and pressure. For example, some people insist that the diver works on the same principle as a submarine whereas others disagree.

A submarine controls its depth by pumping water in and out of special tanks within the submarine. The volume within a submarine stays the same, by virtue of its strong metal hull. When seawater is pumped into the submarine's tanks, the density of the submarine increases and it moves downward. When seawater is pumped out, the submarine density decreases and it becomes more buoyant so it moves upward. Its volume remains the same, but the mass changes by having seawater pumped in and out of the constant volume.

A fish changes its density differently than a submarine. The mass of a fish remains the same, but a fish uses a special bladder within its body to change its density. When the bladder expands, the density of the fish decreases, the fish becomes more buoyant and moves upward. When the bladder shrinks in volume, the fish's density increases and the fish moves downward.

People have different models or viewpoints about how the diver works. How do we settle such differences? Differences in non-science arenas are often settled by such methods as voting, arbitration, negotiation, taking turns, etc. But science is not about opinions; science is about observable fact.

So science disputes are handled differently from most others. Scientists try to resolve disputes by developing an experiment that determines which explanation is right. Scientists try to think up an experiment where Model A predicts one result and Model B predicts a different result. Then the experimental result decides which model is more accurate. Let's look at two models of the diver.

### Model A

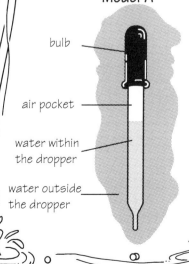

bulb

air pocket

water within the dropper

water outside the dropper

### Model B

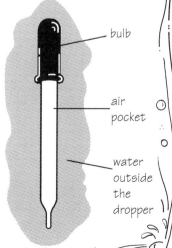

bulb

air pocket

water outside the dropper

Model A says that the diver consists of the dropper, bulb, air pocket in dropper, and the water within the dropper. Model B says that the diver is only the dropper, bulb, and air pocket. Model B says that the water within the dropper is not part of the diver. So both models agree about the dropper, bulb, and air pocket, but they disagree about whether the water within the dropper is part of the diver. Model A states that it is and Model B states that it isn't.

# The Diver's Dilemma: Submarine or Sea Animal?

The difference between these models may seem picky and trivial at first, but it's actually quite important. Model A implies that the diver's volume stays the same, whether the diver is floating, sunken, or suspended in the water tank. Model B implies that the diver's mass is constant but that its volume changes with its depth. When the surrounding water pressure is lowest, the air pocket expands so the diver's volume is high. When the water pressure increases (by squeezing the plastic container), the air pocket shrinks so the diver's volume is small.

These models give very different pictures of the diver's operation. Model A specifies that the diver works like a submarine works, having a constant volume and changing the mass in order to change density, which controls floating and sinking. Model B says that the diver operates differently from a submarine because the diver has constant mass and changes the volume to change the density for the purpose of sinking or floating. Model B says that diver works more like a fish or marine mammal.

Which model is correct? What experiment can distinguish between them? We don't know the answer. Can you think of an experiment to tell?

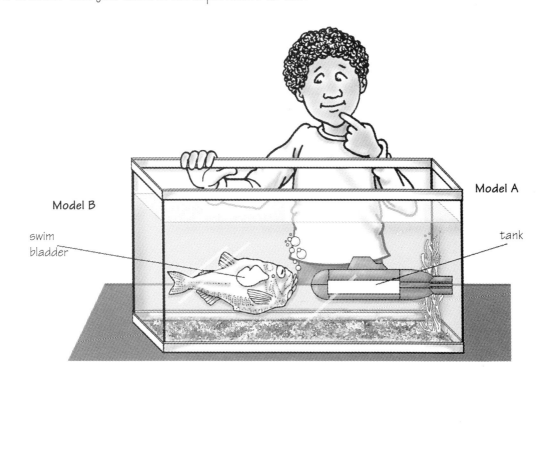

Model B

swim
bladder

Model A

tank

# The Diver's Dilemma: Submarine or Sea Animal?
## Designing a New Experiment

One experiment to help determine whether the diver is a submarine or a fish is to install a "door" near the tip of the dropper. The door defines the inside and outside of the dropper. What's on the bulb-side of the door is "inside" the dropper and what's on the tip side is "outside" the dropper. The door should influence the flow of water in and out of the dropper. By putting a BB or ball bearing in the dropper, water flow is restricted and so the BB functions as a "door." Squeezing the bottle forces water past the BB-door into the dropper, causing the diver to sink. When the bottle is released, water flows out through the BB-door and the diver rises.

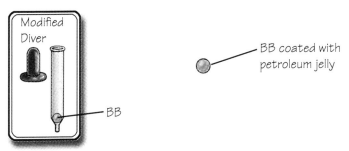

A follow-up experiment is to have a "sticky door" at the dropper's entrance. Coat a BB with a waterproof material that has the texture of a paste. Examples are petroleum jelly or another ointment used to cover a minor wound. The sticky door restricts the flow more than a bare BB, but the diver still works. Squeezing the bottle causes some water to enter the dropper's barrel by momentarily displacing the BB. The sunken diver requires several minutes before enough water escapes the barrel past the sticky door for the diver to rise.

These experiments suggest that the diver is more like a submarine than a fish because the BB defines a diver with constant volume and changing mass, like a submarine. But better experiments are welcome! Can you design an experiment to tell for sure whether Model A or B is correct?

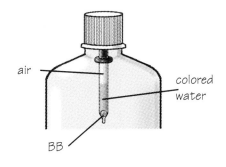

# How Do Sea Animals Dive to Depths of Several Hundred Meters ?

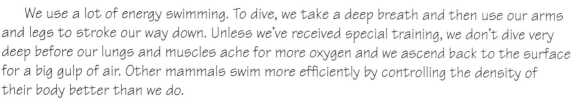

We use a lot of energy swimming. To dive, we take a deep breath and then use our arms and legs to stroke our way down. Unless we've received special training, we don't dive very deep before our lungs and muscles ache for more oxygen and we ascend back to the surface for a big gulp of air. Other mammals swim more efficiently by controlling the density of their body better than we do.

Marine mammals live in the water. Whales, seals, and dolphins have to breathe air like us, but they spend much time underwater. When marine mammals dive, they hold their breath. For shallow dives they use their tails and flippers to move. If they used tails and flippers to propel themselves during deep dives, they would not have enough energy and oxygen to dive very deep. But these animals are known to reach depths as great as 400 meters (over 1200 feet), which is far greater than human divers can reach. How are they able to do this?

Dr. Terrie Williams, a Marine Biologist at the University of California, Santa Cruz, recently headed a team of marine scientists that attached video cameras to several species of deep-diving marine mammals to find out how these animals are able to go to such depths. They found that deep-diving mammals do not swim actively with propulsion by tails and flippers to such depths. Instead, they glide! Gliding requires much less energy and oxygen use than active swimming. They do steer themselves with body motions, but their speed comes from changing their body density so it becomes greater than seawater.

As the animals descend, there is a decrease in lung volume as the lungs gradually collapse due to increasing water (hydrostatic) pressure. For a bottlenose dolphin, complete collapse of the lung (the alveoli or air-carrying cells) occurs when a depth of approximately 70 meters is reached.

The collapse of the lung decreases the volume of the dolphin. Since the mass of the dolphin doesn't change but the volume decreases, the density (mass/volume) of the dolphin increases. As the dolphin's density increases, it sinks and continues active steering. Now the dolphin is gliding down. Such gliding avoids the energy costs of active stroking. The lung collapse also keeps high-pressure gas from getting into their bloodstream, so they don't suffer from the "bends" when ascending. The "bends" is a painful and sometimes fatal condition that occurs when a human diver comes up too rapidly. It is caused by bubbles of nitrogen gas that were trapped in the bloodstream at high pressure when the diver was deep, and then during a rapid ascent, the nitrogen quickly leaves the blood and goes into the body tissues.

The energy-conserving strategy of gliding allows air-breathing sea animals (marine mammals) to increase dive duration and achieve remarkable depths despite limited oxygen availability when submerged. They cannot glide back to the surface because their body density is greater than seawater. Instead they use a stroke-and-glide motion in which they take some power strokes to increase their speed and then glide awhile until their speed drops to about 1 meter per second and then they take another power stroke (like skateboarders). The stroke-and-glide motion is less efficient then the glide during descent, but they have little choice.

The research by Dr. Williams and her team about the diving of marine mammals shows the importance of controlling body density in order to conserve energy and oxygen. However, a mystery that still persists, according to Dr. Williams, is how penguins dive deeply. As birds, their breathing system is different from marine mammals. The diving technique of penguins is unknown and how they might change their body density will probably be discovered by a future researcher.

# The Science and Engineering of The Diver's Dilemma

The "Diver's Dilemma" is a good example of how science and engineering are different and how they support each other. We often rely on technology and the contribution of engineering is apparent, but we aren't always clear on the role of science.

Suppose the submarine was not yet invented and we wanted to invent an underwater vehicle that could dive and ascend like a dolphin. We would carefully observe that a dolphin moves its body in certain ways, and we would learn that the dolphin keeps its mass constant but changes its volume while diving and ascending. We would then try to design a submarine that imitates a dolphin's motions and volume changes, and we would find that we are unable to do this with existing technology. We would probably find that the flexible "skin" of our submarine design would deform to create smaller volume when diving, but the water pressure would then crush our submarine and it would be unable to ascend. A good design for a one-way trip to the bottom! Trying to imitate a dolphin without understanding the science of diving and ascending would lead us to failure.

If we took a more scientific view, we would observe the dolphin and say, "By keeping its mass constant and changing volume, the dolphin dives and ascends by changing its density. It is assisted by its body motions, but the fundamental principle is controlling density. What are other ways to control density?" The science of diving and ascending is about controlling density. The dolphin does it by changing volume while keeping mass constant. Another way is to change mass while keeping the volume constant. Perhaps we can make a rigid shell, unlike the dolphin's flexible skin, to keep the volume constant. Then pump water in and out of holding tanks to control the mass and density of our invention. Eureka! Now we have a viable way to build a submarine with available technology.

By focusing on the science of controlling density, we solved the problem. By focusing on the way a dolphin moves and controls its volume, we did not solve the problem.

A similar example is the airplane. For centuries, humans tried to imitate the flight of birds by focusing on feathers and flapping. During the Industrial Age, humans took a different approach—understand the flight principles of "lift" and "drag" that enable birds and others to fly. Using the scientific principle of lift, the airplane was invented, even though it lacked feathers and it didn't flap!

Moral: If we try to do engineering without understanding the science, we most often end with a soggy mess of feathers, and neither submarine nor airplane.

# The Reverse Diver

## Topic
Pressure in a liquid

## Key Question
How can a Cartesian Diver be made to float from the *bottom* of a container?

## Focus
Students will insert a nonbuoyant Cartesian Diver into a water-filled, flat-sided, plastic mouthwash bottle and observe that when the bottle is squeezed, the diver floats to the top of the bottle.

## Guiding Documents
*Project 2061 Benchmarks*
• *In the absence of retarding forces such as friction, an object will keep its direction of motion and its speed. Whenever an object is seen to speed up, slow down, or change direction, it can be assumed that an unbalanced force is acting on it. [ed. Newton's first law of motion.]*

*NRC Standard*
• *The position of an object can be described by locating it relative to another object or the background.*

*NCTM Standard 2000\**
• *Use common benchmarks to select appropriate methods for estimating measurements*

## Science
Physical science
    density
    pressure

## Integrated Processes
Observing
Comparing and contrasting
Collecting and recording data
Identifying and controlling variables

## Materials
*For each group :*
    flat-sided, plastic mouthwash bottle with cap
    plastic water cup (large enough to float the eyedropper
       in a vertical position)
    eyedropper

## Background Information
*Traditional Cartesian Diver*
    The pressure produced in the water by squeezing the sides of the round, two-liter bottle is transmitted undiminished to every part of the water. Besides the wall of the bottle, the water presses on the bubble of air trapped in the top of the eyedropper. Air is compressible. A given volume of air can be squeezed into a smaller volume. Squeezing the sides of the two-liter bottle reduces the volume of the air bubble. When the volume of the bubble of air is sufficiently reduced, the eyedropper sinks. Releasing the pressure allows the bubble to return to its original size. When the volume of the bubble of air is sufficiently increased, the eyedropper floats.

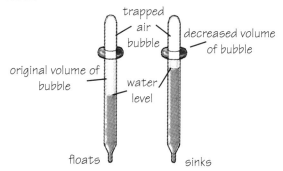

*Reverse Cartesian Diver*
    When the left and right sides of the flat-sided bottle are squeezed, the volume of the bottle is increased. This causes the volume of the air bubble in the eyedropper to increase and the diver floats to the top. Releasing the sides of the flat-sided bottle decreases the volume of the bottle. The volume of the air bubble decreases and the diver sinks.

    To better understand what's going on with the air bubble, let's look at how the increase in pressure produced by squeezing the sides of the two-liter bottle is related to the decrease in the volume (size) of the trapped air bubble.

    Robert Boyle (1627–1691) has been called the founder of modern chemistry. Boyle demonstrated that when he doubled the pressure on a specific quantity of gas, keeping the temperature constant, the volume of the gas was reduced to one-half the original volume (see *B* in the following diagram).

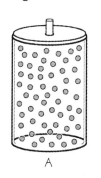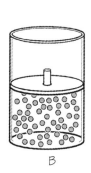

A               B               C

When the pressure was quadrupled, the volume was reduced to one-fourth the original volume (C in the diagram).

As the pressure goes up, the volume goes down. As the volume goes up, the pressure goes down. This relationship between the *pressure* and the *volume* of a gas is known as *Boyle's law*.

## Management

1. Either ask students to bring clean, flat-sided, plastic mouthwash bottles to class or schedule enough time to collect the number of bottles you determine you need to do the activity.
2. Make a Reverse Diver in order to familiarize yourself with the procedure.
3. Be sure the bottles have been cleaned in hot soapy water before distributing them to students.

## Procedure

1. Instruct the students to fill the plastic cup with water. Tell them to experiment to determine the *minimum* amount of water the eyedropper will hold in its barrel and sink to the bottom of the glass.

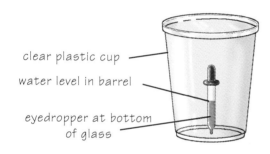

clear plastic cup

water level in barrel

eyedropper at bottom of glass

2. Have students fill the mouthwash bottle with water and then carefully drop the eyedropper into the bottle and observe that it sinks to the bottom. If not, add a little more water to the eyedropper and try again. Instruct the students to screw on the bottle cap.
3. Tell them to squeeze the *front* and *back* sides of the bottle and observe that the eyedropper remains at the bottom.
4. Instruct the students to observe the size of the air bubble in the barrel of the eyedropper and then squeeze the *left* side and the *right* side of the bottle at

the same time. Tell them to record their observations on their student page.

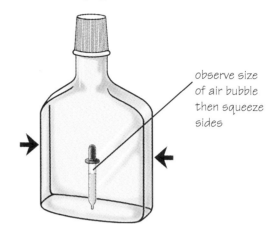

observe size of air bubble then squeeze sides

5. Ask the students to observe the volume of the air bubble in the eyedropper and to record their observations.

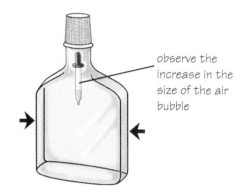

observe the increase in the size of the air bubble

Note: If the eyedropper doesn't float to the top when the sides of the bottle are squeezed, then there's more water in the barrel of the eyedropper than what is required to sink it. Also, be sure students topped off the water in the neck of the bottle before screwing on the cap.

## Discussion

1. What's different about the behavior of the diver in the round, two-liter bottle and the diver in the flat-sided bottle? [The diver in the two-liter bottle floats at the top of the bottle and sinks when the bottle is squeezed. The diver in the flat-sided bottle sinks to the bottom of the bottle and floats to the top when the bottle is squeezed.]
2. What's the same about the two divers? [Squeezing the sides of each bottle changes the volume of the air bubble. Squeezing the two-liter bottle decreases the size (volume) of the air bubble, while squeezing the sides of the flat-sided bottle increases the volume of the air bubble.]
3. What variable determines whether the diver floats or sinks? [The volume of the air bubble in the top of the diver.]

4. Explain why squeezing the side of the flat-sided bottle increases the volume of the air bubble. (Here's a simple method for showing students why squeezing the sides of the flat-sided mouthwash bottle actually *increases* the volume of the bottle. Tape the short edges of two business cards together. The volume contained by the inside faces of the two cards is essentially zero.

two business cards

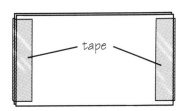

Squeeze the two sides of the cards and a substantial volume is now contained by the inside faces of the cards.)

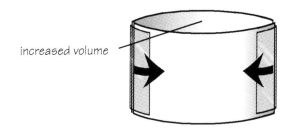

increased volume

5. Compare the trapped air bubble to a coil spring. [When compressed, the air bubble stores potential energy, just like a spring does.]

\* Reprinted with permission from *Principles and Standards for School Mathematics*, 2000 by the National Council of Teachers of Mathematics. All rights reserved.

# The esreveR Diver

Describe what you observe when you squeeze and release the sides of the bottle. If you think it will help, sketch an eyedropper in the bottle diagram.

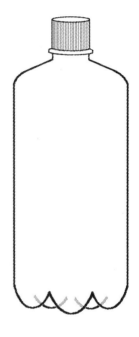

Shade in the barrel of each eyedropper to the fluid level you observed when the eyedropper floats and when it sinks.

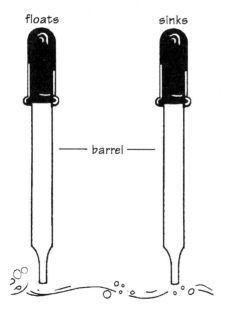

123

# Archimedes

Archimedes (287—212 B.C.) wrote a book titled *On Floating Bodies* which contains what textbooks now call Archimedes' principle.

## Archimedes' Principle

*A body wholly or partially immersed in a fluid will be buoyed up by a force equal to the weight of the fluid that the object displaces.*

It will ease your understanding of Archimedes' principle if the scientific language in which it's stated is translated into everyday language.

A *body* is simply an object—like you, a rock, or a steel ship. *Immersed* means "in." Everyday language usage allows us to be "immersed" in a swimming pool or even a book. You may choose to immerse only your toe in a body of water to check its temperature. You might choose to wade in the water. If you can't swim, you will be careful not to wade to a point where the water level exceeds the level of your waist. If you can swim, you might choose to completely immerse your body by diving and then swimming underwater.

A *fluid* is anything that can flow like water, honey, or even a heavy gas like the carbon dioxide used in monster movies. Like oil on water or gravy on mashed potatoes, fluids flow.

*Buoyed up* means "pushed up." (An object is not "buoyed "down, it's "weighed" down.) *Force* can be defined as a push or a pull on an object. Archimedes' principle describes a force that pushes up on an immersed object. To differentiate this force from other forces, it's called the *buoyant force*. Weight is also a force, but weight always pulls down on an object.

*Displaces* means "takes the place of." Everywhere you go you displace a volume of air equal to the volume of your body (including your hair). Where you now are, air was. Throw a rock in a pond. Where the rock is, water was. Jump into a swimming pool. To whatever level the water reaches on your body, where that part of your body below water level now is, water was.

So, here we have two forces, one pushing up (called the buoyant force) and one pulling down (called weight). The important question related to floating or sinking is, Which force is stronger?

Archimedes' recognized that the buoyant force (the force up) equals the weight (the force down) *of the displaced fluid*. If the force up equals the weight of the object *before the object* sinks below the surface of the fluid, the object floats at a level where the up and down forces are balanced. If not, the object sinks. In either case, the buoyant force is still present.

In the diagram, a cylinder is lowered into a beaker of water (a) and, as shown in (b), it floats.

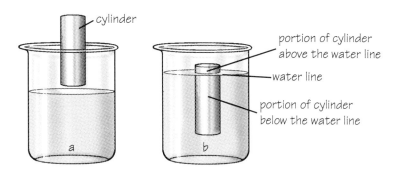

cylinder

portion of cylinder above the water line

water line

portion of cylinder below the water line

a

b

Notice that as the cylinder is lowered, the water level in the beaker rises. Why? Where the cylinder is, the water was (displacement). The water had to go somewhere and the only place it could go was up the sides of the beaker.

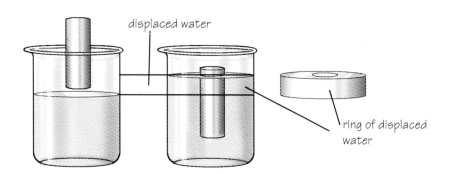

displaced water

ring of displaced water

Using Archimedes' principle, the weight of the displaced ring of water equals the weight of the cylinder. And this weight (a force) equals the buoyant force. Archimedes' principle doesn't tell us *why* the buoyant force is equal to the weight of the displaced water. His principle just states that it is.

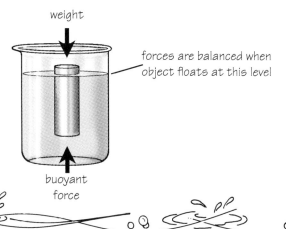

weight

forces are balanced when object floats at this level

buoyant force

# SODA CAN DUNK

## Topic
Buoyant force

## Key Question
How can you observe and measure the *buoyant force* described in Archimedes' principle?

## Focus
Students will investigate the behavior of unopened cans of regular and diet soda suspended from a string and then partly and completely immersed in water. Students will qualitatively and quantitatively explore the buoyant force described in Archimedes' principle.

## Guiding Documents
*Project 2061 Benchmark*
• *The earth's gravity pulls any object toward it without touching it.*

*NRC Standard*
• *If more than one force acts on an object along a straight line, then the forces will reinforce or cancel one another, depending on their direction and magnitude. Unbalanced forces will cause changes in the speed or direction of an object's motion.*

*NCTM Standard 2000\**
• *Understand such attributes as length, area, weight, volume, and size of angle and select the appropriate type of unit for measuring each attribute*
• *Recognize and apply mathematics in contexts outside of mathematics*

## Math
Measurement
    volume
    weight

## Science
Archimedes' principle
    buoyant force

## Integrated Processes
Observing
Collecting and recording data

## Materials
*For each group:*
    clean plastic two-liter bottle
    2 12-ounce unopened cans of the same brand of
        soda, one regular and one diet
    spring scale

## Background Information
Weight is a force and a force pushes or pulls on an object. In this activity, students will explore the buoyant force both qualitatively and quantitatively.

The weight (the downward pull of gravity) of a unopened can of soda suspended on a piece of string from a finger is easily felt. As the can is lowered into a container of water, the pull of the string on the finger is lessened. This diminished pull is easily felt. When partially or totally submerged in water, the can doesn't "feel" as heavy.

Archimedes' principle tells us that a buoyant force acts on any object partially or wholly immersed in a fluid (see *Archimedes' Principle*). This buoyant force is easily observed using the can on a string. Archimedes' principle also states that the buoyant force is numerically equal to the weight of the displaced liquid.

The can of diet soda will float (just barely) in water. The can of regular soda will sink in water. The data for a popular brand of cola recorded in the following table will help us understand why one can of soda floats and the other can sinks. [*Mass* units are grams (g). *Weight* units are gram-force units. One gram-force (gf) unit is the force of gravity (weight) that would act on a mass of one gram. *Volume* units are milliliters (mL).]

| Data | Can of Regular Soda | Can of Diet Soda |
|---|---|---|
| Mass | 386 g | 366 g |
| Weight | 386 gf | 366 gf |
| Volume | 380 mL | 380 mL |

The can of regular soda has a volume of 380 mL (the volume listed on the can (355 mL) is the volume of the fluid *contents* of the can). When it's submerged in water, the can displaces 380 mL of water. One mL of water has a mass of one gram and a weight of one gram-force. According to Archimedes' principle, the buoyant force is equal to the *weight of the displaced water*. Therefore, the buoyant force equals 380 gf. But the weight of the can of regular soda *exceeds* 380 gf. The buoyant force is weaker than the weight of the can and the can of regular soda moves downwards, in the direction of the stronger force, until it is stopped by the bottom of the container. A similar analysis reveals that the buoyant force of 380 gf exceeds the weight of the can of diet soda. The can of diet soda therefore floats at a level where the weight of the volume of water displaced by the submerged portion of the can equals 366 gf. The buoyant force and the weight balance *before* the top of the can reaches the surface of the water. Therefore, the can floats.

The floating and sinking of the cans of soda can also be understood from the density perspective.

$$density(diet\ can) = \frac{366\ \frac{g}{}}{380\ mL} = 0.96\ \frac{g}{mL}$$

$$density(regular\ can) = \frac{386\ \frac{g}{}}{380\ mL} = 1.02\ \frac{g}{mL}$$

The density of water is one gram per mL. The density of the diet soda is slightly less than the density of water so the can of diet soda floats in water. The density of regular soda is slightly greater than the density of water so the can of regular soda sinks. Note that these are average densities since they include the different densities of the aluminum can, the soda, and the air pocket in the can.

## Management
1. Ask students to bring empty, clean two-liter bottles to class.
2. Cut the neck off an empty two-liter bottle. Tape the two-liter bottle scale (see *Two-Liter Bottle Volume Scales* page) to the side of the bottle. Align the zero mark on the scale with the circular indentation line near the bottom of the bottle.

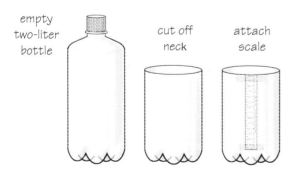

empty two-liter bottle    cut off neck    attach scale

Make one two-liter bottle with scale for each group of students.

3. Purchase the regular and diet cans of soda packaged in the plastic neck-rings. Carefully cut the cans from the neck rings. Be sure to leave the plastic collars intact. Punch a small hole in the rim of each collar

and tie a 8-inch length of string to the collar. Tie a finger loop in the end of each string.

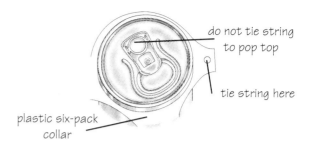

plastic six-pack collar    do not tie string to pop top    tie string here

4. Divide the students into groups of two or three.
5. You may choose to have your students complete only *Part One*, the qualitative investigation, of this activity. For *Part Two*, decide whether to provide students the data or have the students measure the weights and volumes of the two cans. Use a spring scale with capacity of at least 400 grams and an accuracy of a few grams, preferably one gram.
6. Provide paper towels to clean up spillage.

## Procedure
*Part One: Qualitative Investigation*
1. Distribute one water container (filled to the 600 mL level), one can of regular and one can of diet soda (with strings attached), and the student pages to each group.
2. Instruct the students to loop the end of the string around an index finger (near the tip) and lift the can into the air so that they can feel its weight. Tell them that the weight they feel is indicated by the "X" on the scale shown on the student page.
3. Have them lower the can into the water container until the can is approximately half submerged and estimate the change in weight, lighter or heavier, by drawing a vertical line on the scale.
4. Tell them to lower the can until it is completely submerged and to estimate any change in weight by placing a vertical line on the scale to the left or right of the "X."
5. Ask the students to describe any changes they felt in the weight of the can of regular soda as it was lowered into the water.
6. Instruct the students to repeat the process for the can of diet soda.
7. Have the students compare their investigation of the can of regular soda with their investigation of the can of diet soda.
8. Ask the students to describe how their weight changes when they are swimming.

*Part Two: Quantitative Investigation*
1. Have students complete the data table. [Either provide students the values of the weights and volumes or let them make the measurements themselves. A spring scale can be used to measure

the weights of the regular and diet cans of soda and the regular can of soda can be submerged in the two-liter container of water and its volume measured by observing how much water it displaces (see diagram below).]

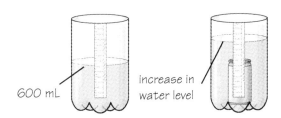

600 mL        increase in water level

2. Tell the students to read the statement of Archimedes' principle.
3. Have the students determine and then record the volume of water displaced by the regular can of soda and its weight.
4. Ask the students to determine and record the buoyant force acting on the submerged can of regular soda.
5. Tell the students to record the difference between the weights of the can of regular soda and the buoyant force acting on the submerged can.
6. Using the results from the previous question, have the students describe why the can of regular soda sinks in water.
7. Instruct the students to determine and record the buoyant force on the floating can of diet soda.
8. Knowing the buoyant force on the floating can of diet soda, ask students to determine and record the volume of water the floating can of diet soda displaces.
9. Using the weight of the can of diet soda and the known buoyant force, have the students describe why the can of diet soda floats.

**Discussion**
*Part One*
1. How did the weight of the can of regular soda when half submerged in water compare to its weight in air? [lighter]
2. How did the weight of the fully submerged can of regular soda compare to its weight in air? [even lighter]
3. How did the weight of the can of diet soda when half submerged in water compare to its weight in air? [lighter]
4. How did the weight of the can diet soda when it's just about to float compare to its weight in air? [even lighter]
5. Compare your investigation of the can of regular soda with your investigation of the can of diet soda. [Both cans feel lighter when in the water. The regular can of soda sinks but the diet can floats. I can still feel a tug on my finger when the

regular can of soda is below the top of the water but not resting on the bottom of the container. At the point where the can of diet soda is no longer sinking, and begins to float, I can barely feel a tug on my finger.]

6. How do you think your weight changes when you go swimming? [I feel much lighter in the water. If I relax, on my back, I can just barely float. If I let all of the air out of my lungs, I start to sink.]
7. Why do you think astronauts train for space walks by practicing their activities underwater in large swimming pools? [Having their space suits connected to the surface of the swimming pool by an air hose allows the astronauts to practice their maneuvers under water which simulates the weightless environment of outer space.]

*Part Two*
1. What volume of water does the regular can of soda displace? [380 mL]
2. What is the weight of the displaced water? [380 gf]
3. What is the buoyant force on the submerged can of regular soda? [380 gf]
4. What is the difference between the weight of the can of regular soda, in air, and the buoyant force acting on the submerged can? [386 gf – 380 gf = 6 gf]
5. Why does the can of regular soda sink? [The downward weight of the can exceeds the upward buoyant force by 6 gf. Therefore, the can sinks to the bottom of the container.]
6. What is the buoyant force on the floating can of diet soda? [366 gf]
7. What volume of water does the can of diet soda displace? [366 mL]
8. Why does the can of diet soda float? [The buoyant force of 366 gf balances the 366 gf weight of the can of diet soda *before* the top of can reaches the surface of the water. Therefore, the can floats.]

**Extension**
Have students repeat the investigation but substitute the spring scale for their finger. They can then quantify the weights when the cans are half and fully submerged.

Archimedes' Principle applies to buoyancy in gases as well as liquids. A medium-size adult man weighs 75kg and displaces about 75 liters of air, which has a density of 1.3 g/L. What is the buoyancy force pushing up on the man and how does it compare with his weight pushing down. [About 100 gf buoyancy, which is about 0.1% of his weight.]

* Reprinted with permission from *Principles and Standards for School Mathematics*, 2000 by the National Council of Teachers of Mathematics. All rights reserved.

# Two-Liter Bottle Volume Scales

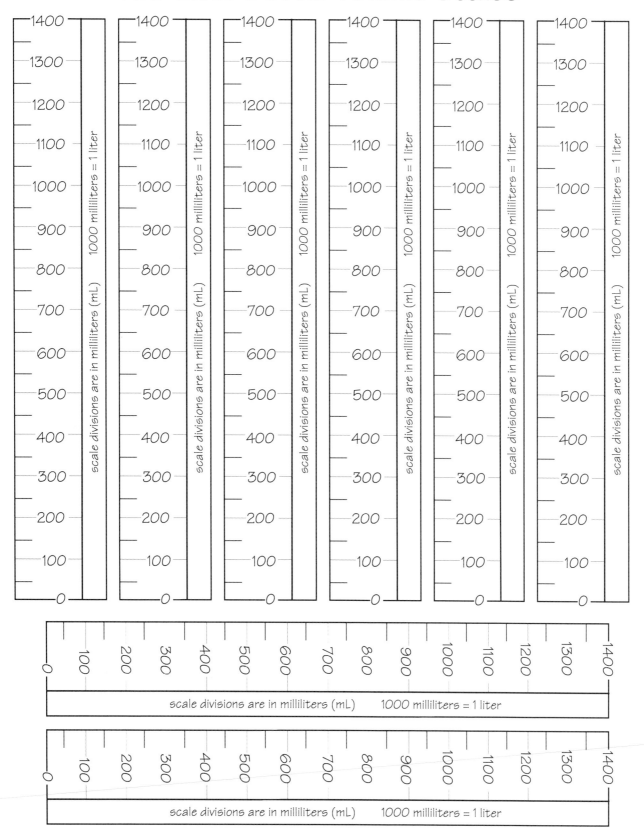

# SODA CAN DUNK

1. Compare the weight of the can of regular soda in air, when half submerged, and when fully submerged.

2. Describe any changes you felt in the weight of the can of regular soda as you lowered it in the water.

3. Compare the weight of the can of diet soda in air, when half submerged, and when fully submerged.

4. Describe any changes you felt in the weight of the can of diet soda as you lowered it in the water.

5. Compare your investigation of the can of regular soda with your investigation of the can of diet soda.

6. Describe how you think your weight changes when you go swimming.

## Can of Regular Soda

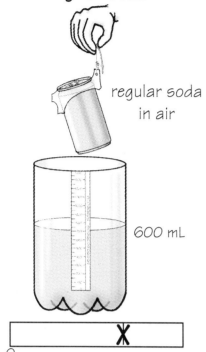

regular soda in air

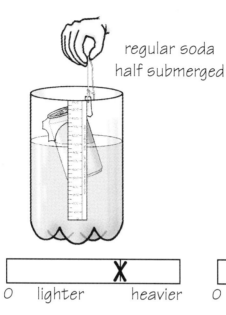

regular soda half submerged

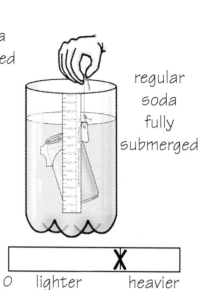

regular soda fully submerged

600 mL

| | X | |
|---|---|---|
| O | | |

(**X** = weight of can in air)

| | X | |
|---|---|---|
| O | lighter | heavier |

| | X | |
|---|---|---|
| O | lighter | heavier |

## Can of Diet Soda

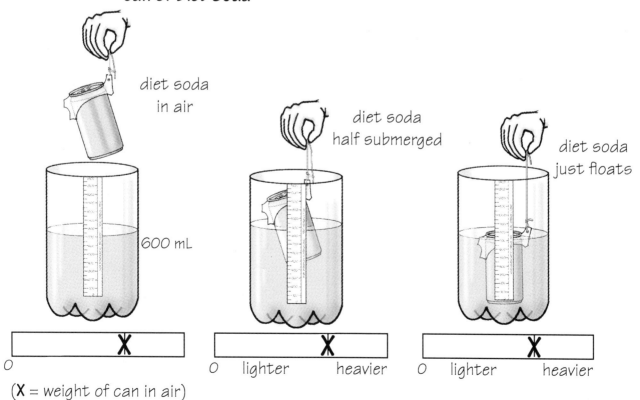

diet soda in air

diet soda half submerged

diet soda just floats

600 mL

| | X | |
|---|---|---|
| O | | |

(**X** = weight of can in air)

| | X | |
|---|---|---|
| O | lighter | heavier |

| | X | |
|---|---|---|
| O | lighter | heavier |

# SODA CAN DUNK

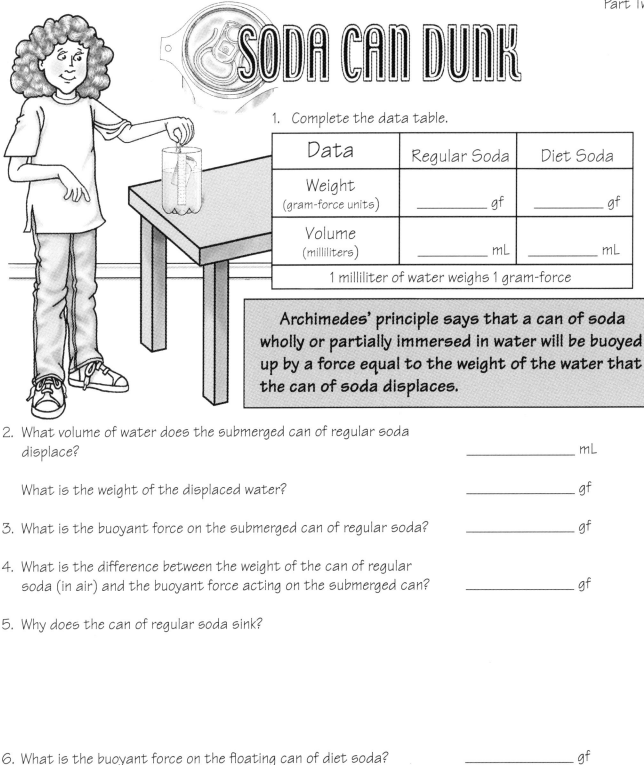

1. Complete the data table.

| Data | Regular Soda | Diet Soda |
|---|---|---|
| Weight (gram-force units) | _____ gf | _____ gf |
| Volume (milliliters) | _____ mL | _____ mL |
| 1 milliliter of water weighs 1 gram-force | | |

Archimedes' principle says that a can of soda wholly or partially immersed in water will be buoyed up by a force equal to the weight of the water that the can of soda displaces.

2. What volume of water does the submerged can of regular soda displace?

_____ mL

What is the weight of the displaced water?

_____ gf

3. What is the buoyant force on the submerged can of regular soda?

_____ gf

4. What is the difference between the weight of the can of regular soda (in air) and the buoyant force acting on the submerged can?

_____ gf

5. Why does the can of regular soda sink?

6. What is the buoyant force on the floating can of diet soda?

_____ gf

7. What volume of water does the can of diet soda displace?

_____ mL

8. Why does the can of diet soda float?

# Geoffrey I. Taylor (1886 – 1977)

G. I. Taylor is credited as the co-discoverer of Rayleigh-Taylor Instability, although he actually rediscovered it over fifty years after Lord Rayleigh's work. Taylor was an English scientist, sailor, and inventor who made significant contributions in many fields where fluids are important. Having fun and overcoming a challenge were important in both his work and personal life. He discovered several fluid effects that now bear his name and the name of a co-discoverer, like Rayleigh-Taylor Instability. Another example is the Taylor-Couette Instability that occurs in spinning fluids.

Before he became a well-known researcher in fluid instabilities, he studied weather. He was a meteorologist, a weatherman, for a few years. After the *Titanic* struck an iceberg and sank, he was a member of an expedition that reported on icebergs in the North Atlantic Ocean.

His favorite form of recreation was sailing. As a sailor he found that a common problem was dealing with raising and lowering a heavy boat anchor. His solution was to invent a new type of anchor. He used the knowledge gained by years of experimenting with fluids to develop an anchor that was effective yet lightweight. Boats today continue to use the design that was invented in 1933.

During World War II, Taylor applied his knowledge of fluid instabilities to underwater explosions and to development of the atomic bomb. Scientists in the Manhattan Project at Los Alamos needed an understanding of Rayleigh-Taylor Instability to make the bomb work, and this physics continues to be an active area of research in the science of weapons. The phenomenon was not called "Rayleigh-Taylor Instability" until about fifteen years after World War II ended. It was called "Taylor Instability" during the 1950s because scientists forgot about Raleigh's earlier research.

# Lord Rayleigh (John William Strutt, 1842 – 1919)

Unlike most scientists today who focus their work in a particular area of science, Lord Rayleigh's interests were varied and far-ranging. He made important contributions in studies of sound, light, and fluids. For example, he discovered that light scattering from tiny particles in the air causes the sky to appear blue. It's now called "Rayleigh Scattering."

He did lots of experiments with fluids. The "Rayleigh-Taylor Instability" is only one of several discoveries. When he was about 30 years old, he built a laboratory next to his home. Today most science is done in companies or universities, but Rayleigh did his wonderful experiments in his own small private laboratory.

Lord Rayleigh was awarded the Nobel Prize in Physics in 1904. It's one of the biggest prizes for physics research. Ironically, he did not win it for his work in sound or light; he won the Nobel Prize for helping discover the element argon, which occurs in very, very small amounts in the atmosphere. Discovering an element is more like chemistry research than physics, but Rayleigh was good at that, too.

He became good at physics after his college education. During college he was especially strong in mathematics. He later used his math skills to make theories about his physical discoveries. He saw more clearly than most scientists how science and math can be combined. Having a strong math background helped him understand physics phenomena and explain it more effectively to others.

# Professor Sheila Widnall (1938 –    )

When Professor Sheila Widnall and some engineering students observed a moving smoke ring strike a wall, they had different ideas about what was happening. They all saw the smoke ring become wavy as it got near the wall. The students thought the waviness has something to do with the smoke ring hitting the wall. Professor Widnall thought that the waviness was something that happens to smoke rings and didn't depend upon the wall. She was right. She did some calculations about the "instability" of a vortex ring and showed that it becomes wavy.  A smoke ring is a type of vortex ring. (The ring of a food-coloring drop in the *Flow Fingers* activity is another type of vortex ring.) In the field of fluid dynamics, the person who discovers an effect often gets their name attached to the label for that effect. So the waviness of a vortex ring is the "Widnall Instability."

Professor Widnall has made tremendous contributions to science beyond discovering how vortex rings behave. As a professor at the Massachusetts Institute of Technology (M. I. T.), she teaches classes in the engineering department. She has helped many students have successful college experiences and she helps them launch their own work careers. Also, she has done much research about fluids other than vortex rings, and she has received many honors for her superb work.

From 1993 to 1997 Ms. Widnall was Secretary of the Air Force. She is the first woman to head a branch of the U. S. military.

Both her father and mother got her interested in a science and math career. When she was young, she and her father did a lot of projects like building, painting, rewiring, and pouring concrete. Her mother was a social worker, and so young Sheila learned that a woman can pursue a career and a family, and do a great job at both.

# Glossary for *Spills and Ripples*

**Archimedes' Principle:** A floating object is buoyed up by a buoyancy force equal to the weight of displaced liquid. The object floats because this buoyancy force is greater than the object's weight. A submerged object also experiences an upward (buoyancy) force equal to the weight of displaced liquid, but the object sinks because its weight is greater than the buoyancy force. (*Soda Can Dunk*)

**barometer:** a type of manometer for measuring the pressure of the air around us. (*Open-tube Manometer*)

**Boyle's Law:** For a gas in a container at fixed temperature, an increase in pressure causes a decrease in the gas volume, and a decrease in pressure causes an increase in volume.

**brackish water:** water that is salty, but less salty than sea water (*Brackish Water*)

**brine:** salty water

**buoyant force, buoyancy:** an upwards force acting on any object partially or fully submerged in a fluid like water or air. (*Soda Can Dunk*, *Delicate Diver*)

**Cartesian Diver:** a small container of water and air (like an eyedropper) that is open at the bottom and closed at the top, suspended in a larger container of water (like a one-liter plastic bottle) that can be slightly pressurized or depressurized. The diver is nearly (i.e., neutrally) buoyant, and the pressurization or depressurization causes it to sink or float. (*Delicate Diver, The Reverse Diver*)

**conduction:** a means of heat transfer from one material to another when the two materials are in direct contact

**convection:** vertical motion of fluid caused by temperature differences. The vertical motion transports heat, salinity, or other fluid properties. Typically, heating the bottom of a liquid container causes the warmed liquid to flow upward. Convection can be started by Rayleigh-Taylor Instability.

**density:** the ratio of mass to volume. Density is a property of a substance. The density of water is 1 $g/cm^3$ (gram per cubic centimeter). The mass of water occupying a volume of 1 cubic centimeter is 1 gram. Cooking oils have a density about 0.9 $g/cm^3$. Sugar and salt solutions have densities greater than 1.0 $g/cm^3$. "Lightness" and "heaviness" are non-scientific ways to describe the density of a substance relative to another.

**diffusion:** The process in which small solid, liquid, or gas particles spontaneously move through each other. Thermal agitation causes the particles to move.

**diffusive mixing:** where mixing of fluids occurs by diffusion

**fluid:** a gas or liquid. A substance that flows. *Spills and Ripples* deals only with gases and liquids, not granular fluids like flowing salt or sugar.

**fluid interface:** the boundary between a gas and another gas, a gas and a liquid, a liquid and another liquid. Some examples are: the boundary between car exhaust and fresh air, the surface of a pond and the boundary between salt water and fresh water.

**hydrometer:** an instrument for measuring specific gravity of liquids

**instability:** when little ripples (or perturbations) become larger and larger

**interface:** where two different materials touch

**hydrometer:** an instrument for measuring specific gravity of liquids

**manometer:** an instrument for measuring fluid pressure, usually relative to atmospheric pressure

**Pascal's Principle:** The pressure applied to a gas or liquid in a container acts in all directions on the gas or liquid, and the pressure is transmitted everywhere in the container.

**perturbation:** a disturbance of a balanced or smooth state. A small ripple on an otherwise smooth water surface is a perturbation. The scientific research literature about Rayleigh-Taylor Instability uses "perturbation" in the same sense that *Spills and Ripples* uses "ripple."

**pressure:** the ratio of force to the area subjected to the force. The force must be perpendicular to the surface.

**radiation:** The transmission of energy by electromagnetic waves.

**Rayleigh:**

Lord Rayleigh (John William Strutt) studied fluid instabilities and many other science subjects. His investigations in 1880 included the effect that became known as Rayleigh-Taylor Instability about 80 years after his work. He also discovered why the sky is blue, an effect known as "Rayleigh Scattering." (1842-1919)

**Rayleigh-Taylor**
**Instability:** the growth of ripples (i. e., perturbations) at an interface between two fluids (i. e., gases or liquids) when the higher-density fluid is on top. The growing ripples become finger-like projections or plumes of one fluid into the other. It usually leads to pouring or spilling. It is "driven" by gravity.

**ripple:** wave-like perturbation or disturbance at a liquid/gas interface, like ripples on a pond

**salinity:** saltiness

**salt fingers:** vertical flows in the ocean caused by the competition between heat diffusion and salt diffusion

**specific**
**gravity:** the ratio of a material's density to the density of water. Specific gravity has no units. The specific gravity of water is 1.00. The specific gravity of cooking oils is about 0.9.

**stratified:** layers of fluid that are stacked by virtue of their density. The higher-density layer is below the lower-density layer.

**surface**
**tension:** skin-like behavior of the surface of a liquid

**Taylor:** G. I. Taylor is the co-discoverer of Rayleigh-Taylor Instability (1886-1977)

**Widnall:** Sheila Widnall studied the instabilities of vortex rings. She teaches engineering classes at the Massachusetts Institute of Technology. (1938-   )

**Widnall**
**Instability:** how a "vortex ring" (e.g., smoke ring or drop of liquid falling through a surface of another liquid) of fluid breaks up by developing about four to eight ripples that grow into fingers

# The AIMS Program

AIMS is the acronym for "**A**ctivities **I**ntegrating **M**athematics and **S**cience." Such integration enriches learning and makes it meaningful and holistic. AIMS began as a project of Fresno Pacific University to integrate the study of mathematics and science in grades K-9, but has since expanded to include language arts, social studies, and other disciplines.

AIMS is a continuing program of the non-profit AIMS Education Foundation. It had its inception in a National Science Foundation funded program whose purpose was to explore the effectiveness of integrating mathematics and science. The project directors in cooperation with 80 elementary classroom teachers devoted two years to a thorough field-testing of the results and implications of integration.

The approach met with such positive results that the decision was made to launch a program to create instructional materials incorporating this concept. Despite the fact that thoughtful educators have long recommended an integrative approach, very little appropriate material was available in 1981 when the project began. A series of writing projects have ensued and today the AIMS Education Foundation is committed to continue the creation of new integrated activities on a permanent basis.

The AIMS program is funded through the sale of this developing series of books and proceeds from the Foundation's endowment. All net income from program and products flows into a trust fund administered by the AIMS Education Foundation. Use of these funds is restricted to support of research, development, and publication of new materials. Writers donate all their rights to the Foundation to support its on-going program. No royalties are paid to the writers.

The rationale for integration lies in the fact that science, mathematics, language arts, social studies, etc., are integrally interwoven in the real world from which it follows that they should be similarly treated in the classroom where we are preparing students to live in that world. Teachers who use the AIMS program give enthusiastic endorsement to the effectiveness of this approach.

Science encompasses the art of questioning, investigating, hypothesizing, discovering, and communicating. Mathematics is a language that provides clarity, objectivity, and understanding. The language arts provide us powerful tools of communication. Many of the major contemporary societal issues stem from advancements in science and must be studied in the context of the social sciences. Therefore, it is timely that all of us take seriously a more holistic mode of educating our students. This goal motivates all who are associated with the AIMS Program. We invite you to join us in this effort.

Meaningful integration of knowledge is a major recommendation coming from the nation's professional science and mathematics associations. The American Association for the Advancement of Science in *Science for All Americans* strongly recommends the integration of mathematics, science, and technology. The National Council of Teachers of Mathematics places strong emphasis on applications of mathematics such as are found in science investigations. AIMS is fully aligned with these recommendations.

Extensive field testing of AIMS investigations confirms these beneficial results.

1. Mathematics becomes more meaningful, hence more useful, when it is applied to situations that interest students.
2. The extent to which science is studied and understood is increased, with a significant economy of time, when mathematics and science are integrated.
3. There is improved quality of learning and retention, supporting the thesis that learning which is meaningful and relevant is more effective.
4. Motivation and involvement are increased dramatically as students investigate real-world situations and participate actively in the process.

We invite you to become part of this classroom teacher movement by using an integrated approach to learning and sharing any suggestions you may have. The AIMS Program welcomes you!

# AIMS Education Foundation Programs

## A Day with AIMS®

Intensive one-day workshops are offered to introduce educators to the philosophy and rationale of AIMS. Participants will discuss the methodology of AIMS and the strategies by which AIMS principles may be incorporated into curriculum. Each participant will take part in a variety of hands-on AIMS investigations to gain an understanding of such aspects as the scientific/mathematical content, classroom management, and connections with other curricular areas. *A Day with AIMS®* workshops may be offered anywhere in the United States. Necessary supplies and take-home materials are usually included in the enrollment fee.

## A Week with AIMS®

Throughout the nation, AIMS offers many one-week workshops each year, usually in the summer. Each workshop lasts five days and includes at least 30 hours of AIMS hands-on instruction. Participants are grouped according to the grade level(s) in which they are interested. Instructors are members of the AIMS Instructional Leadership Network. Supplies for the activities and a generous supply of take-home materials are included in the enrollment fee. Sites are selected on the basis of applications submitted by educational organizations. If chosen to host a workshop, the host agency agrees to provide specified facilities and cooperate in the promotion of the workshop. The AIMS Education Foundation supplies workshop materials as well as the travel, housing, and meals for instructors.

## AIMS One-Week Perspectives Workshops

Each summer, Fresno Pacific University offers AIMS one-week workshops on its campus in Fresno, California. AIMS Program Directors and highly qualified members of the AIMS National Leadership Network serve as instructors.

**For current information regarding the programs described above, please complete the following:**

## The AIMS Instructional Leadership Program

This is an AIMS staff-development program seeking to prepare facilitators for leadership roles in science/math education in their home districts or regions. Upon successful completion of the program, trained facilitators may become members of the AIMS Instructional Leadership Network, qualified to conduct AIMS workshops, teach AIMS in-service courses for college credit, and serve as AIMS consultants. Intensive training is provided in mathematics, science, process and thinking skills, workshop management, and other relevant topics.

## College Credit and Grants

Those who participate in workshops may often qualify for college credit. If the workshop takes place on the campus of Fresno Pacific University, that institution may grant appropriate credit. If the workshop takes place off-campus, arrangements can sometimes be made for credit to be granted by another institution. In addition, the applicant's home school district is often willing to grant in-service or professional-development credit. Many educators who participate in AIMS workshops are recipients of various types of educational grants, either local or national. Nationally known foundations and funding agencies have long recognized the value of AIMS mathematics and science workshops to educators. The AIMS Education Foundation encourages educators interested in attending or hosting workshops to explore the possibilities suggested above. Although the Foundation strongly supports such interest, it reminds applicants that they have the primary responsibility for fulfilling *current* requirements.

---

## *Information Request*

Please send current information on the items checked:

_____ *Basic Information Packet* on AIMS materials

_____ *AIMS Instructional Leadership Program*

_____ *AIMS One-Week Perspectives* workshops

_____ *A Week with AIMS®* workshops

_____ Hosting information for *A Day with AIMS®* workshops

_____ Hosting information for *A Week with AIMS®* workshops

Name _____ Phone _____

Address _____
Street                                                  City                                    State        Zip

---

# We invite you to subscribe to *AIMS*!

Each issue of *AIMS* contains a variety of material useful to educators at all grade levels. Feature articles of lasting value deal with topics such as mathematical or science concepts, curriculum, assessment, the teaching of process skills, and historical background. Several of the latest AIMS math/science investigations are always included, along with their reproducible activity sheets. As needs direct and space allows, various issues contain news of current developments, such as workshop schedules, activities of the AIMS Instructional Leadership Network, and announcements of upcoming publications.

*AIMS* is published monthly, August through May. Subscriptions are on an annual basis only. A subscription entered at any time will begin with the next issue, but will also include the previous issues of that volume. Readers have preferred this arrangement because articles and activities within an annual volume are often interrelated.

Please note that an *AIMS* subscription automatically includes duplication rights for one school site for all issues included in the subscription. Many schools build cost-effective library resources with their subscriptions.

## YES! I am interested in subscribing to *AIMS*®

Name _____   Home Phone _____

Address _____   City, State, Zip _____

Please send the following volumes (subject to availability):

| | | | | | | |
|---|---|---|---|---|---|---|
| _____ | Volume VII | (1992-93) | $15.00 | _____ Volume XII | (1997-98) | $30.00 |
| _____ | Volume VIII | (1993-94) | $15.00 | _____ Volume XIII | (1998-99) | $30.00 |
| _____ | Volume IX | (1994-95) | $15.00 | _____ Volume XIV | (1999-00) | $30.00 |
| _____ | Volume X | (1995-96) | $15.00 | _____ Volume XV | (2000-01) | $30.00 |
| _____ | Volume XI | (1996-97) | $30.00 | _____ Volume XVI | (2001-02) | $30.00 |

_____**Limited offer: Volumes XVI & XVII (2001-2003) $55.00**
(Note: Prices may change without notice.)

**Check your method of payment:**

☐ Check enclosed in the amount of $_____

☐ Purchase order attached (Please include the P.O.#, the authorizing signature, and position of the authorizing person.)

☐ Credit Card   ☐ Visa   ☐ MasterCard   Amount $ _____

Card # _____   Expiration Date _____

Signature_____   Today's Date _____

Make checks payable to **AIMS Education Foundation**.
Mail to *AIMS*® Magazine, P.O. Box 8120, Fresno, CA 93747-8120.
Phone (888) 733-2467   FAX (559) 255-6396
**AIMS Homepage: http://www.AIMSedu.org/**

# AIMS Program Publications

## GRADES K-4 SERIES

Bats Incredible!
Brinca de Alegria Hacia la Primavera con las Matemáticas y Ciencias
Cáete de Gusto Hacia el Otoño con la Matemática y Ciencias
Cycles of Knowing and Growing
Fall Into Math and Science
Field Detectives
Glide Into Winter With Math and Science
Hardhatting in a Geo-World (Revised Edition, 1996)
Jaw Breakers and Heart Thumpers (Revised Edition, 1995)
Los Cincos Sentidos
Overhead and Underfoot (Revised Edition, 1994)
Patine al Invierno con Matemáticas y Ciencias
Popping With Power (Revised Edition, 1996)
Primariamente Física (Revised Edition, 1994)
Primarily Earth
Primariamente Plantas
Primarily Physics (Revised Edition, 1994)
Primarily Plants
Sense-able Science
Spring Into Math and Science
Under Construction
Winter Wonders

## GRADES K-6 SERIES

Budding Botanist
Crazy About Cotton
Critters
El Botanista Principiante
Exploring Environments
Fabulous Fractions
Mostly Magnets
Ositos Nada Más
Primarily Bears
Principalmente Imanes
Water Precious Water

## GRADES 5-9 SERIES

Actions with Fractions
Brick Layers
Brick Layers II
Constructores II
Conexiones Eléctricas
Down to Earth
Electrical Connections
Finding Your Bearings (Revised Edition, 1996)
Floaters and Sinkers (Revised Edition, 1995)
From Head to Toe
Fun With Foods
Gravity Rules!
Historical Connections in Mathematics, Volume I
Historical Connections in Mathematics, Volume II
Historical Connections in Mathematics, Volume III
Just for the Fun of It!
Looking at Lines
Machine Shop
Magnificent Microworld Adventures
Math + Science, A Solution
Multiplication the Algebra Way
Off the Wall Science: A Poster Series Revisited
Our Wonderful World
Out of This World (Revised Edition, 1994)
Paper Square Geometry: The Mathematics of Origami
Pieces and Patterns, A Patchwork in Math and Science
Piezas y Diseños, un Mosaic de Matemáticas y Ciencias
Proportional Reasoning
Ray's Reflections
Soap Films and Bubbles
Spatial Visualization
Spills and Ripples
The Sky's the Limit (Revised Edition, 1994)
The Amazing Circle, Volume 1
Through the Eyes of the Explorers:
    Minds-on Math & Mapping
What's Next, Volume 1
What's Next, Volume 2
What's Next, Volume 3

For further information write to:
AIMS Education Foundation • P.O. Box 8120 • Fresno, California 93747-8120
www.AIMSedu.org/ • Fax 559•255•6396

# AIMS Duplication Rights Program

AIMS has received many requests from school districts for the purchase of unlimited duplication rights to AIMS materials. In response, the AIMS Education Foundation has formulated the program outlined below. There is a built-in flexibility which, we trust, will provide for those who use AIMS materials extensively to purchase such rights for either individual activities or entire books.

It is the goal of the AIMS Education Foundation to make its materials and programs available at reasonable cost. All income from the sale of publications and duplication rights is used to support AIMS programs; hence, strict adherence to regulations governing duplication is essential. Duplication of AIMS materials beyond limits set by copyright laws and those specified below is strictly forbidden.

## Limited Duplication Rights

Any purchaser of an AIMS book may make up to *200 copies* of any activity in that book for use at *one school site*. Beyond that, rights must be purchased according to the appropriate category.

## Unlimited Duplication Rights for Single Activities

An individual or school may purchase the right to make an unlimited number of copies of a single activity. The royalty is $5.00 per activity per school site.

Examples:  3 activities x 1 site  x $5.00 =  $15.00
9 activities x 3 sites x $5.00 = $135.00

## Unlimited Duplication Rights for Entire Books

A school or district may purchase the right to make an unlimited number of copies of a single, *specified* book. The royalty is $20.00 per book per school site. This is in addition to the cost of the book.

Examples:
5 books        x 1 site    x $20.00  =  $100.00
12 books      x 10 sites x $20.00  = $2400.00

## Magazine/Newsletter Duplication Rights

Those who purchase *AIMS*® (magazine)/*Newsletter* are hereby granted permission to make up to 200 copies of any portion of it, provided these copies will be used for educational purposes.

## Workshop Instructors' Duplication Rights

Workshop instructors may distribute to registered workshop participants a maximum of 100 copies of any article and/or 100 copies of no more than eight activities, provided these six conditions are met:

1. Since all AIMS activities are based upon the *AIMS Model of Mathematics* and the *AIMS Model of Learning*, leaders must include in their presentations an explanation of these two models.
2. Workshop instructors must relate the AIMS activities presented to these basic explanations of the AIMS philosophy of education.
3. The copyright notice must appear on all materials distributed.
4. Instructors must provide information enabling participants to order books and magazines from the Foundation.
5. Instructors must inform participants of their limited duplication rights as outlined below.
6. Only student pages may be duplicated.

Written permission must be obtained for duplication beyond the limits listed above. Additional royalty payments may be required.

## Workshop Participants' Rights

Those enrolled in workshops in which AIMS student activity sheets are distributed may duplicate a maximum of 35 copies or enough to use the lessons one time with one class, whichever is less. Beyond that, rights must be purchased according to the appropriate category.

## Application for Duplication Rights

The purchasing agency or individual must clearly specify the following:
1. Name, address, and telephone number
2. Titles of the books for Unlimited Duplication Rights contracts
3. Titles of activities for Unlimited Duplication Rights contracts
4. Names and addresses of school sites for which duplication rights are being purchased.

NOTE: *Books to be duplicated must be purchased separately and are not included in the contract for Unlimited Duplication Rights.*

The requested duplication rights are automatically authorized when proper payment is received, although a *Certificate of Duplication Rights* will be issued when the application is processed.

Address all correspondence to:  **Contract Division**
**AIMS Education Foundation**
**P.O. Box 8120**
**Fresno, CA  93747-8120**

www.AIMSedu.org/
Fax 559•255•6396

## DATE DUE